LADDER
to
LEADER

*My Journey from Failure to Fire
to Financial Freedom*

RYAN D. LARSON

Calling Card Books
Burnsville, NC

www.CallingCardBooks.com

Cover design, interior design, and editing
by Calling Card Books.
www.CallingCardBooks.com
Burnsville, North Carolina

Cover Photo By: Aaron Blackburn, www.aaronblackburn.com

First Edition
Paperback ISBN: 978-1-7354845-1-8
E-book ISBN: 978-1-7354845-2-5

Library of Congress Control Number: 2021918372

CONTENTS

PROLOGUE

SITTING HERE IN THE SPRING of 2020 as the world goes into lockdown because of COVID-19, a worldwide pandemic, I've had a lot of time to think. Looking back on my road to owning FirstLine Financial, LLC, a Registered Investment Adviser Firm, I find myself wondering how in the world I got here. I owe part of this success to my wife Kate, who's my rock and business partner in the firm. The rest is me, but I don't fit the profile of a typical successful financial adviser. Most of those guys went to a famous business college and my parents often wondered if I would even graduate from high school. Things weren't simple back then and I always felt like the black sheep at home. I was always stressed by my older brother and two younger sisters constantly saying that I scared them. During my elementary and high school years, I was that kid whose test scores weren't anything to brag about. I had way too much energy and was put in Resource classes for slow learners. Hearing that you're not smart like the other kids takes a toll, so I became known as a good fighter. Yes, I got in trouble – a lot. My parent's goal was for me just to graduate so that I could get a job somewhere and move out on my own.

I graduated from high school and enrolled in a local community college, but I wouldn't say I liked school during this period. I spent a few lost years going from job to job, hanging out with the wrong people, and getting into more trouble than I care to think about. During that time, on at least one occasion, I considered taking my own life. I seriously had a lot of things to figure out to get my life in order but wasn't finding a whole lot of answers.

Thankfully, through an intriguing twist of fate that my mom thinks was divinely guided, I decided to become a firefighter, which is not a simple process. As of today, I've been a firefighter and loving the job for over 20 years, but there's always been something inside of me – what my wife calls "a fire inside that drives me." This thing deep inside me says, *Ryan is this all there is for you?* That fire inside may be the reason that, while I was still a booter – a trainee that mops the floors while the Captain and more experienced guys watch T.V. – I got interested in investments. FirstLine Financial, LLC is my "days off" job still to this day, and a lot of my FirstLine clients work the fire line right next to me. Managing the savings of these hardworking men and women, who put their lives on the line daily, is an enormous responsibility that our firm takes very seriously.

We're proud to serve first responders. Blue-collar workers are the heartbeat of this country. Today I own a white-collar business while still doing a blue-collar job. This combination makes for a very busy, hectic life that's demanding both physically and mentally, and I love every minute of it. I've always had goals and aspirations, the fire in my belly. It's about being of service, a mindset and commitment that every firefighter must possess to do what we do. Maybe that burning desire to help others comes from my black sheep days or possibly from the tragedies witnessed in my firefighting career.

Whatever it is, in my early forties, I'm proud of my happy, beautiful family, Kate, our daughter Mia, and son Bryson, and the clients who entrust their life savings to me. I'm honored to work with brothers and sisters in the firehouse and truly cherish the deep bonds, built over time, with my parents, brother Rob, and sisters Jennifer and Aimee. The reason I've put time into writing this personal story to share with you is because what we've created at FirstLine Financial, LLC works. We developed a process that earned a Service Mark from the U.S. Patent and Trademark Office for the patented process we use to serve our clients. That certificate is framed and hangs proudly in our office because earning it is no small step, and we achieved it in five short years! I wrote this book to help you, the reader, understand that there are many ways you can save and grow your money to live better, retire comfortably, or leave a legacy.

Life has taught me many things over the years, and the most important lesson I've learned is that trust is everything in any kind of relationship. First responders learn to trust their training and their team because lives depend on us. We've got to do our job and do it right in challenging situations where we often can't even see each other through the smoke and flames. That unshakable, steadfast trust comes from living together, learning together, and working together in unfathomable situations and all kinds of circumstances. This book is my way of spending time with you, so you can get to know who I am and trust what I tell you about what I know and how FirstLine Financial, LLC can help you take care of your financial life.

I share personal stories in this book – like the times I should have died on a call but didn't. I also share stories about my journey to achieve financial adviser accreditation, which forced me to take – and pass – many very difficult tests, something I failed at miserably when I was in school. But, most importantly, I introduce important information about investing to help you understand how you can gain your financial freedom, no matter how old you are or how much money you start with.

CHAPTER 1

WHERE IT BEGAN

I REMEMBER WHEN I WAS a kid and heard a noise outside one night that scared me a little. I peeked out the window and saw a man next to the 1987 Ford pickup that my dad absolutely loved and still talks about to this day. I got out of bed, shook off sleep, went into my parents' room, and let my father know that someone was messing around near his truck. Dad flew out of bed in his underwear, rushed outside and yelled at a man siphoning gas out of his beloved truck. I remember he came back inside yelling, "Barb, we need to get the kids out of this place."

That happened in Tempe, a town on the outskirts of Phoenix, Arizona, and wasn't the best of neighborhoods back then. It's home to Tempe Town Lake, one of Arizona's most visited places today. According to the City, the lake was built by damming the dry Salt River in 1977, the year I was born. We lived in a rented duplex along the seasonal dry riverbed. As kids, we enjoyed that area tremendously. It was basically our playground growing up.

My parents didn't have a lot of money, so with two boys and a girl on the way, they rented one side of that duplex down the block from my grandparents' home. Our side of the house butted up against the Salt River riverbed, and Mom liked being there because her parents lived down the street from us. My grandparents helped take care of us, so Mom was able to work at Sky Harbor Airport in Phoenix to help with expenses doing floral design at a flower cart.

Mom and Dad got married when they were young. My mother was only nineteen when I was born. My father enlisted in the Air Force right after my older brother was born to provide for our family. They were dedicated to doing the best for us kids but never had a lot of money, so we'd spend a lot of time doing outdoor activities and camping, especially after my sister was born. We all slept in the back of my dad's truck which we kids loved. To this day, my sister loves to go camping, though it takes hours for her to get ready. She always has to put on makeup and go through her endless supply of clothes. But she's still an outdoors girl at heart, and every year on her birthday all she wants is to go camping.

When Mom was expecting Aimee, the youngest, my folks knew we had outgrown the 850 square foot duplex, and we moved to our first house in Chandler. Our new home was a bit farther to the southeast of Tempe but still in Arizona, and we spent the next 18 years growing up making many fond memories there. But even after the move to Chandler, I felt like the black sheep of the family. I tell this story to people who know how close I am to my brother and sisters now. It helps them understand my "outsider" status back then.

I think it was my grandparent's 50th anniversary when we drove to Laughlin, Nevada, on the California border near the Mojave desert south of Las Vegas. We all piled into our family's good old Astro Van and drove the 250 or so miles northwest.

I remember my mom and dad going out to get a bite to eat when we finally got into Nevada. I was eight or nine years old, so my brother was nine or ten. My parents went out and left my brother in charge and told us all to stay in the room. People used to do that back then, so it wasn't anything new to us. Whenever my parents left us at home, my two sisters and brother acted like they were scared of me, and it wasn't a game. I was a rambunctious kid who wanted to wrestle whenever the adults were gone, like my friends at school did, but my siblings just wanted to talk and watch T.V. I remember watching other brothers fight and wrestle and it looked fun. I thought that was normal, but my siblings did not want any part of roughhousing with me. Back being left in the room on our trip, it wasn't long before Rob took both girls into the bathroom and locked the door, saying he was scared that I would do something to them. I never understood what I did to scare them so much or why my brother was so intimidated by me. I have asked him why they were so scared of me, now that we're older and closer than I expected us to be given our early years.

"Ryan," he said, "I always felt like you were going to attack us."

My brother was different than any of my friends at school. He confused me. Back then, I had no connection with my sisters, but they were very close to my brother who seemed to have some sort of power over them.

I could hear him and my sisters in the bathroom at that casino saying, "Ryan's gonna kill us. He's evil. Stay away from him."

After a while that gets to you. Feeling upset that they had locked the door, I remember beating on it and saying, "Rob, let me in. I'm not going to do anything."

I knew I had to focus on something else, so I began watching T.V. until suddenly, my brother ran out of the bathroom and into the hallway. I was a skinny, scrawny kid and didn't have a shirt on, just my shorts when I chased him out of the room. I thought he was hiding in the vending machine area near the ice when all of a sudden, he runs past me back into the room and locks that door. With no shirt on, I banged on the door in the hallway of the casino, "Rob, let me in." My brother did not let me in and when I get agitated, I start walking and don't think about anything. I just keep moving my feet.

I was eight or nine years old and didn't know what to do, so I just walked. If someone tried to tell me to do something, I was the kind of kid that did the exact opposite. That night, I started by walking down our hallway which turned into the casino where I saw lots of slot machines and poker tables. There I was, a little eight or nine-year-old boy traipsing through the slot machines and gaming tables with no shirt on, not really sure where to go or what to do. In my mind I was looking for my parents, and soon enough, a security guard was standing over me.

"You know, son, you can't be in here," he said. "You have no shirt, no shoes, and you're underage." I felt lost, helpless, and scared. I didn't know what to do and no one seemed to want to help me, so I tried to go back to the room but had a hard time finding it and saw an exit sign. I decided to go that way. I walked out the exit doors, but right then, I was overwhelmed with fear and quickly turned around to get back in. But it was too late as the doors abruptly closed before my eyes. I knew right then that I couldn't get back in without a key. Realizing what I just got myself into, I felt defeated. I forced myself to shrug it off and turned around to face my reality, which was nothing I had ever seen before. Imagine the first time you're seeing the Las Vegas Strip with its surreal, fast-paced, glitzy atmosphere blanketed with neon lights that seem to go for miles and miles. Now imagine seeing it for the first time as an 8-year-old, standing half-naked, frozen in what felt like an eternity. The cold night air took my breath away, and the bottoms of my feet ached with what felt like 1000 needles. Immediately, I started shivering from the chill. As I stared out into the cold darkness of the parking lot, my heart sank. I was afraid for my future. I was lost without anyone to call. All I had was courage to push me forward. The parking lot looked somewhat familiar. I remembered coming into the casino's lot with my head out the window, taking in the sites – something I always did on road trips – especially when we went up north to the mountains. I enjoyed taking in the cool, fresh mountain air and letting the wind breeze through my face and hair. But in my current reality, I kept walking. Somehow, don't ask me how; I found our Astro Van and finally felt relieved to see something familiar. I decided the only place I could hide without getting in trouble with security guards, where I could protect myself if anyone tried to mess with me, was on top of the van. It had stairs on the back and a luggage rack on top, so I climbed up and nestled in as best I could. I vividly remember shivering from the cold metal on my bare skin and crying up there all by myself. I knew that I was in a horrible situation during the worst trip ever. I was up there probably an hour and a half or two hours until finally falling asleep.

I woke up from my perch atop the Astro Van with my dad pulling on my ankle. My parents had gotten back to the room and found out what happened, so Dad headed back out and looked around the casino. When he did not see me anywhere, call it fatherly instinct, he went straight to the Astro Van.

Photo: Astro Van, Ryan with siblings Aimee, Jennifer, Rob

"What are you doing, Ryan."

"Dad, Rob locked me out of the room. I had nowhere to go. I tried to find you in the casino, but I couldn't find you."

I was still crying when my dad picked me up. My big, strong Air Force Master Sergeant carried me back to the room because I was too cold to walk. When we got back, he gently tucked me into bed, bringing an end to that traumatic experience. My dad was quite the disciplinarian, so being gently tucked into bed by him was a nice change from my normal routine of getting spanked with his big leather belt. Trust me. I felt the sting from the large cowboy buckle on that belt whenever there was a serious infraction of the rules.

CHAPTER 2

FAILURE TO LAUNCH

MY PARENTS WERE INCREDIBLY SUPPORTIVE but never very focused on academics. Though she got pregnant very young, Mom had guidance from her parents and earned her high school diploma, but my dad didn't finish high school or get his diploma with his class, but he made sure to get his GED when he could. He quit school and took responsibility for the care of my mom and their future child – my brother Rob. I've always respected him for that. My dad has always been proud of being a blue-collar guy, and there was never a lot of emphasis on academics and getting good grades. *Ryan, get C's so you can get through and get a diploma,* was the extent of my parental guidance about academics.

As time went on, I wanted to play football and my parents were one-hundred-percent behind me being involved in athletics of any kind. That was an excellent way for me to use up my abundant energy. Because I couldn't sit still at school, they hoped football would be my ticket to a promising future. Dad coached the Pop Warner team which was my first intensive training. Dad made me stand up to the whole team. Every player would run at me, hit my shoulder pads, trying to knock me down, and then step aside for the next person and the next and the next until everyone had their turn. I took hits from as many as twenty guys, one at a time. Other times I would be on one side of the field with the rest of the team on the other side, and they would all try to tackle me at once. Twenty or thirty people were all racing down the field toward me. I would juke them out, which means I'd get around them and run to the opposite end zone for the touchdown. I was small yet athletic, agile, and fast on my feet, and those guys didn't scare me.

Dad pushed me. I played defense which he coached, and offense. My dad wanted me to be the best football player on his team. I was one of the Pop Warner stars, but I never got a break and sometimes felt pressure from everyone to perform, especially my dad. I remember a guy named Aaron and another named Jessie, friends of mine on other teams who were two of three top players. I rounded out the top three. Whenever we'd compete on the field for a game, at least one person in the crowd could be heard saying, *Ryan Larson's on that team.* I was always the running back and team captain. I consistently scored, sometimes four to five touchdowns per game. Because of my success in Pop Warner, Dad's goal was to improve my athletic abilities by always throwing unusual drills at me. My Dad was not the head coach, but the head coach's son also played. Both of us felt the pressure and expectation of pulling up the entire team.

There were a lot of drills focused on just the two of us. The coaches constantly worked on improving our athletic abilities, and at times, it felt like they didn't focus on the rest of the team. Interestingly, no one seemed to complain about that. I believe my dad's goal was for me to be a professional football player, and it became my goal, too. I think that's what every kid who plays youth football plans to do if they enjoy playing. With my Pop Warner star status and the athletic abilities that earned me that status, I thought my pro-football dream might actually come true.

Puberty didn't hit me until my junior year of high school, and I remember going out for the freshman football team. A lot of kids much bigger than me had the same idea, and I only weighed 98 pounds my freshman year. I was very small and not built for football. I knew right then that my size would be an issue in high school.

After the first year of high school football, my coach pulled me aside. He told me that I was too small and would likely not go anywhere in football, but he had other ideas for me. He saw something in me that I didn't and became the driving force in the direction I would take moving forward. With football season coming to an end, he mentioned that a friend I went to junior high with told him that I dominated wrestling in seventh grade. My only loss was to the state champion that year, who still happens to be one of my dearest friends.

Back then, I couldn't stand him. He was a year older, undefeated, and this red-headed kid that everyone feared. Our paths would cross again almost a decade later, and I still had the same opinion of him. Eventually, we struck up a friendship that has lasted over 20 years. It's funny how someone that you thought you would never connect with can become one of your best friends for life. I've learned that sharing your story and connecting with people, being honest about life's realities – good or bad – is really important. You never know what life has in store for you, and that unexpected friend could say or do the right thing just when you need it.

I finished every wrestling season qualifying for the state championship but never ranked until my senior year where I ranked #1 for state but finished my high school wrestling career in third place. I loved wrestling, it got me small scholarship offers my senior year, but more than that, it allowed me to let out a lot of the feelings that were being locked away inside me. I was so used to Dad's presence during Pop Warner, but now I felt his absence everywhere, which was hard on me. He was on active duty in the U.S. Air Force during that time and was away for long periods of time. He completed two tours in his 20-year career. When I was four, Dad was stationed in Korea for a year and deployed to Iraq during the Desert Storm crisis in 1991, so he missed wrestling matches during those years. I think that may be why I had so much success then. I wanted to give my dad something to look forward to. He was the driving force for performing very well in wrestling while he was in Iraq. During our weekly phone calls, I would tell him about every match. Those chats gave me the drive and motivation to win. I wanted him to share in those wins, to feel a part of the team while he was away. Dad wrote to me promising time together when he got home, but that didn't happen. My Dad and I have a great relationship, but it's definitely been a work-in-progress.

My parents were busy raising four children and just trying to put food on the table. As a father raising my own childen, I realize now it had to be really hard on them. I can't imagine being so young themselves, trying to do what they did when they had four young kids. Now I understand what they were up against more than ever. Mom worked a lot while Dad was away, and before he deployed to Iraq, he told me that I had to be the man of the house. I realize now that trying to be the man of the house put pressure on me, and I got into lots of fights at school, often to protect my brother.

I also went through a weird phase; I was angry at the world and I'm not really sure why. It could have been from not seeing my dad for two years during junior high during such a crucial stage of development. I was angry before he deployed. I didn't want him to go and didn't know how to handle it. These days we are truly best buds and go hunting a lot. In nature, away from everyone and everything, those father-son hunting trips are where we connected and mended some of the issues we had.

That high school football coach who said I was too small to succeed in football was also the wrestling coach. When he proposed wrestling over football, I had my sights set on becoming a star running back in the NFL and giving up football made no sense to me. I wanted to say no, but at home that night I discussed it with my parents. When we were done talking, I called my friend who had told coach about my wrestling successes in middle school and asked why the heck he was shattering my NFL dreams. I listened to what coach, my parents, and my friends thought and decided I would give high school wrestling a shot. After four years of wrestling, two of which I was team captain, my wrestling days were over as soon as I graduated.

I always thought my athletic ability would take me somewhere in this world, but that was not in the cards for me. Living with my parents wasn't always easy. After I graduated from high school, they expected me to do one of two things while living under their roof: I had to work or go to school. I decided to do both. First, I needed money to party, and second, I wanted to meet girls. Where else can you get both at one time? College, of course! I needed a job and had a few along the way. Some jobs I quit out of frustration, sometimes feeling that I knew more than my boss. One boss asked me to use the forklift, which I'd never been trained on, to move a huge electrical junction box that seemed to outweigh the lift. I was not going to risk my safety or the company's property. I didn't, and of course, that was the end of that job. I felt like a round peg in a square hole in many of those jobs, but I think things happen for a reason and would just move on to the next job.

I was working as a personal trainer at an LA Fitness Center when it burned to the ground. I thought, *Oh great, I'm out of a job again.* So, I got another job as a cashier at Home Depot. One day while I was at my register, a kid lit a fire in the paint aisle, and it erupted. I saw black smoke – which means the fire is hot, it's volatile, and it's dangerous. I immediately started going up and down three aisles, including paint, to help customers find the exit and piled out of the building along with them and other employees. I watched the firefighters pull up in their red fire trucks and run through the big sliding glass doors to battle the flames as a lot of thick, black smoke billowed out. I knew they probably couldn't see anything once inside because the smoke was overwhelming even outside. I was captivated watching them get through anything that was in their way. It was clear that they knew exactly what to do and how to do it. They got into the enormous commercial building full of combustible material in no time. I could not believe what I was seeing! All I could think was *those guys are amazing.* These two fires are the *divine intervention* I mentioned in the Prologue.

I was still attending community college when that happened, and soon I found myself unmotivated. I felt that my life was going nowhere, that I had no purpose. I remember breaking down in total frustration when I got home one day and talked to my mom, still crying, and told her how lost I felt. Mom is an amazing woman who eventually fought off a form of cancer that takes many lives at this young age. So, when I shared my frustration, she had no pity for me. Both parents raised us with discipline and tough love, but I always felt they were harder on me than the others. I came to realize that was because I was, in a way, the man of the house while Dad was deployed. He had pulled me aside before deploying and reminded me that I had two younger sisters to watch over and an older brother that needed me. I protected them at school, especially Rob, so I did feel like the man of the house. Sometimes that role was hard on me, but there were times that I felt invincible.

I remember years before talking to my mom about feeling lost and unmotivated. The family was driving to Salt Lake City, Utah, in our minivan, and I fought with my siblings, which wasn't unusual. I remember Dad pointed his finger at me like I was causing all the ruckus. I got so mad that I told my parents to let me out of the car because I would walk the rest of the way! I think we were going to meet my cousin Penny for her wedding and had another 200 miles to go. Surprisingly, my dad called my bluff and pulled over on the side of the road and said, *get out.* Being a stubborn kid, I jumped out and started walking down the busy highway. I was a strong-headed boy that wasn't scared to do anything to prove a point. Maybe my parents saw that in me, too. As I look back, those moments really started to define who I was and who I was to become.

But getting back to the day when I watched firefighters working on a common goal at the Home Depot store, when I got home from work I broke down and poured my heart out to her, my mom told me she found something that I might be interested in when I got home from work. She had seen a listing about an opportunity to be in an Explorer program for kids who want a career in the Chandler Fire Department. My eyes lit up! *Maybe,* I thought, *this is my opportunity to put all those team-building skills and athletic abilities I learned throughout my childhood to use in one place.* My answer to her was, "Let's do it!"

CHAPTER 3

WELCOME TO THE SHOW

AS MY MOM AND I pulled into the parking lot on the first night of Chandler's Fire Explorer Program, looking out the car's window I saw two tall buildings. I wondered what they were and soon found out they were burn towers used to teach firefighters search and rescue drills. Also, other trucks from around the city would come together for multi-company training drills and use those burn towers. These training programs are where instructors begin to separate those who have the strength and stamina to make it as a firefighter. One of the first challenges faced was climbing the five flights of stairs required to ascend the tower. We had to race up with approximately 65 pounds of gear that consist of our helmet, bunker pants and jacket, self-contained breathing apparatus (SCBA), and a tool, sometimes an ax or other tools of the trade. We would also sometimes carry a dummy weighing an additional 100-pounds over our shoulder and race to the top.

I met the captain in charge of the Explorer program walking into the training room that first night. He asked my name and if I had what it takes to be a firefighter. I was not really sure what he meant, but definitely sure this is what my future should be, so I said, *Absolutely!* For the next three years, I spent many hours in the hot Arizona sun loading and unloading fire hoses, hooking them up to hydrants, and performing other fire-related tasks that would prepare me for the job. I also spent many hours performing community activities and doing ride-alongs to learn how to be a good citizen of the community, not just a firefighter. In this job you quickly realize the general public sees firefighters as the people to call during emergencies, no matter what kind of situation or crisis they have. We gear up and show up during what is probably the worst time in that person's life and spend many hours servicing the community's needs. That might be teaching kids about fire safety, pool awareness, CPR, or just performing tours at the fire station. I wasn't aware of all of those ordinary, routine activities of the job when I started. But through my Explorer training, I realized that serving my community is what I would love the most about this job. Although running into a burning building is pretty exciting as well, especially for someone like me who loves a challenge!

When it was finally time to take the test that would show the Chandler Fire Department, I was ready to wear their uniform and protect the community where I grew up. I was almost unable to control myself. Wanting to show the examiners how badly I wanted the job, I was one of the first explorers to pick up an application. What better way to prove my goal of becoming a Chandler firefighter than being the first in line? For the next two months, I prepared myself for the exam that every candidate must take to become a firefighter because I knew it was not easy. My mom's brother tested for the Phoenix Fire Department thirty years ago when he was in his twenties. He told me that, back then, there were ten thousand applications received to fill five to eight openings. The test is not an easy thing to pass – it challenges your body and your mind. As I met other firefighters, they told me that it's not unusual for individuals to take this test six or seven times before passing it or just giving up. I heard about one guy who took the test for <u>ten</u> years. Now, that's dedication to a goal!

I had faced the fact that I wasn't a good test taker when I was in school, so I spent hours and hours studying. It became clear to me that I needed a tutor to help me prepare for the math section because, in school growing up, math was my weakest subject. As a kid, I was in a program called Resource, which involved being put in special classes for slow learners. I would be pulled out of my regular classroom for certain subjects like math and reading comprehension because I couldn't grasp things like the other kids. I got teased by my classmates about Resource and usually don't talk about it because it was very embarrassing back then. I remember coming home from school and bawling because I felt so different, an outsider at school, just like I was at home with my siblings. I had to focus intensely to barely pass; my school years were a long and difficult road. But I wanted to be a firefighter so much that I figured out how to apply myself. Eventually, I started getting in the 90th percentile on tests. Passing the written test is required to be considered for employment, so I had a lot to learn about math and so much more. The hiring process is layered, and it is tough.

The first thing every applicant has to pass are a written exam and skills test—only those who score in the high 90's move on to be interviewed. The next step is passing the Candidate Physical Ability Test (CPAT) physical exam, which consists of eight events designed to show whether the candidate has the physical ability and strength to perform essential jobs at a fire scene. If readers are interested in finding out more, there is a link in the footnotes to the Phoenix Fire Department CPAT test criteria and their hiring process . If a candidate passes the CPAT within 10 minutes and 20 seconds, they are moved on to the Oral Board Interview, which consists of two rounds. Then, depending on the circumstances, you may have to do an additional interview with the Chief.

Math and Reading Comprehension were part of the written test, and I was worried because I was too active and busy with sports to read a lot. But when I set my mind on something, I am a very hard worker, so I studied more than I ever had in my life. I think this was when I began to think of myself as an intelligent guy who just hadn't learned how to take tests. I had street smarts from my early years and figured out how to get book smarts, too. I had to because testing only happens every two or three years. I could not keep floating endlessly through unfulfilling jobs, and the fire department might have five thousand applications for only twenty positions. As I've said before, the screening process is brutal because fire chiefs want the smartest, most athletic, and most dependable people. Those attributes are particularly necessary in the heat of the fire, and they want the best interviewers because firefighters deal with the general public on a regular basis.

CHAPTER 4

LIFE TEACHES

THIS WAS THE TURNING POINT in life. I began to understand that *what you think you are is what you become.* So on the day of the exam, I was ready and felt confident. I had worked hard on the grinder – what the training academy is called – and felt like I spent an ample amount of time hitting the books, too. I arrived that morning to take my test and walking up to the testing site, I saw a line of candidates wrapping around the building. To say I was overwhelmed is an understatement! After waiting in line with thousands of applicants, I signed in and walked into the testing room to see rows and rows of people from all walks of life <u>already</u> sitting there waiting to take that same test. I was barely 21 years old and used the full allowable time – three and a half hours – to complete the test. I was one of the last people to turn in my test.

I walked out of the building feeling a little defeated, knowing my test-taking abilities were not my strong suit. Having just taken my first fire test, I knew there was still a lot to learn, but hopeful that I performed well enough to pass. The next step would be the physical aptitude part of the test – my strong suit. I thought I would shine and was eager to get to that point in the screening process. Dad's Pop Warner coaching, which put me through the gauntlet many times, had proven to be helpful during all of the grinder's physical challenges. I was ready to go, but the next two weeks were extremely stressful. I knew living at home, especially now that I was out of high school, on my parent's modest income at the time that had to support my younger sisters and me, wasn't easy on any of us. I stayed focused the best I could, mostly by going to the Explorer program every Tuesday and Saturday morning.

Two weeks later, I came home from work and there was an envelope from the city addressed to me. I was excited and could not control myself, so I ripped open the envelope, pulled out a letter, and read: *Mr. Larson, we're sorry to inform you that you didn't pass the written portion of the exam.* I was devastated! I didn't know what to do, and it felt terrible. I broke down because I had let myself and my parents down. We all go through moments in life when it feels that things can't possibly get any worse, and this was one of those moments. But it's during those tough times – I truly believe –when we figure out who we are. I had to do something, so I put on my running shoes. Like

Forrest Gump, I started running as fast and as far as I could! Running has helped me through many difficult moments in my life. It allows me to push through the pain and test my limits. After forcing myself to run further than I had ever run before, I came home with a clear head. At that point in my life, I love running. When I got to the point where I couldn't run anymore, I'd always find some breakthrough. Seeing those test results, I was primed for a breakthrough. Though the pain of failure was still there, I felt rejuvenated. Somehow, I knew this was my destiny and failing this test would not stop me.

I hit the books harder than I ever had in my life. That first test showed me some of the weaknesses that I had to work on. Staying committed to the Explorer program with mentors who were already full-time firefighters allowed me to improve in areas that would determine whether I would advance to the next round. So, I jumped right back into the routine of studying. I dug into my books and spent two days a week at the training facility and on the grinder to prepare myself for another testing opportunity with the Chandler Fire Department.

While waiting for the next Chandler Fire Department test to come around, I refined my test-taking skills by testing with other fire departments around the valley. I got hired by the much smaller Sun Lakes Fire Department reserve program before I could retake Chandler's test. Sun Lakes took in three to five people as backups to their regular full-time firefighters. It wasn't a volunteer firefighter position. It was a part-time paid opportunity to network, learn, practice, and build a Fire Fighter resume, so I took it. If someone was sick, we were on their dial sheet. I never knew when I'd get a call saying, *Hey Ryan, someone called in sick for this shift. Can you work it?*

I built up a good reputation while still taking tests for other fire departments. I was building my reputation through everything I was doing and tested for the Chandler Fire Department again while in their Explorer program. While working at GNC, I got a call from my mom telling me I had a letter from Chandler Fire Department. I got really excited and asked my boss if I could go home to find out what the letter was about. Everyone at GNC knew I wanted the job, so she said yes. I rushed home, ran inside the house and immediately opened the letter. *Congratulations, Ryan Larson. You have officially been accepted into the Chandler Fire Department Intern program.* I was so excited and hugged my mom and dad! I was crying and feeling good until I called Human Resources as the letter said. It took a minute of me giving her all of my information before she told me that my letter was a mistake. It turns out they accepted another Ryan Larson, not me.

So my testing, networking, and waiting continued. I had put myself back into the Chandler Fire Department testing process once more, and when the day came, I was full of emotions walking into one more test. I knew this time it was different. I had done everything possible to prepare and finished fairly quickly this time. When I stood up and looked around, there were tables full of people with their noses in the test. I knew I had probably just written my ticket to the CPAT I passed the written and CPAT test and would have the opportunity to sit in front of some of the men and women I'd spent hours with on ride-alongs and at the academy for the interview process.

A few weeks later, I received a call saying that I was accepted into a five-week intern academy. This intern academy was how the department selected applicants that would best fit the culture and tradition of the Chandler Fire Department. As an intern, for five weeks we did timed runs, pass/fail tests, evolutions on the grinder, and fireground survival and save-your-own drills, all of which were used to rank my group of interns. An intern's rank in the group determined who was best equipped to be accepted into the Chandler fire family.

Around that time, I also tested for the City of Phoenix Fire Department. This was my third time, two of which I made it all the way through the testing process. Not too long after the third test, I got a call from Phoenix saying, *Congratulations, Ryan, you came out number one on our list. Would you like a job?* Though my heart was connected to the Chandler Fire Department, the largest fire department in Arizona had just made me a job offer. Though people kept telling me that I did really well on the Chandler test, I accepted the offer from Phoenix. Ironically, the next day the Chandler Fire Department called and offered me a job, too. I was offered jobs two days in a row from two of Arizona's biggest fire departments. That was the biggest compliment and confidence booster that I'd ever had.

When that call from Phoenix came in offering me a position as a full-time firefighter, I opened my mouth but had trouble finding the words to respond. It was something that I had been looking forward to hearing for a long time. Of course, I said yes and started my career with the Phoenix Fire Department by going through a twelve-week academy to further my knowledge and experience and learn what the job would entail. Those twelve weeks were the most fun I'd had in my life. That was where I met and became friends with incredible people, some who I still call my closest friends today. One of the guys who went through the Phoenix Fire academy with me had been my arch enemy that beat me in wrestling in 7th grade, and he would go on to have an 18-1 record his 8th-grade year. He added one loss to what would have been an undefeated record that year, and now we worked side by side. You never know where life will take you.

I was determined to do my best, and as I said before, the grinder reminded me of when Dad coached me in football. I learned to be ready for anything and do whatever was necessary to succeed. So, I think it was the tenth week of that twelve-week academy, we're nearing the end and it's getting really exciting. By this time, we're not pretending anymore. They're throwing real-life situations at us, and you can't be worn out – digging deep is the only option. We're very close to graduation and have to get certified on a list of skills. One we call "taking a hydrant," meaning you have to unscrew the hydrant, attach a hose, open the hydrant, and get water to the firetruck in one minute and thirty seconds. Another skill is donning all your turnout in thirty seconds or less. Turnouts include your heavy fire-resistant, waterproof bunker pants, bunker boots, and bunker coat, as well as your helmet, Nomex fire-resistant hood, fireproof gloves, and your SCBA bottle and mask, all in thirty-five seconds or less.

One of the skills that every firefighter has to learn is how to properly throw up a ladder consisting of a 12foot and 24-foot-ladder. Possibly the most nerve-racking is knowing how to handle the 35-foot-ladder, which is massive, difficult to deploy, and can raise up to the third story of a building. The ladder is stored on the ladder truck and has three sections that extend and collapse to fit in the ladder truck. Most ladder trucks also have an aerial ladder, a permanent part of the truck that's only operated by certified engineers. The 35-foot-ladder is a pass/fail evolution and needs to be passed before graduating and must be deployed within one minute and 15 seconds. It takes three firefighters to carry and raise the 35-foot extension ladder because it is really heavy and very awkward.

The time had come for my crew to get signed off on this beast of a ladder, and we're all pretty beaten up and tired at this point of the process. For almost twelve weeks, we'd been waking up at three-thirty in the morning every morning, running one and a half miles, and doing the skills course. From early morning until the end of each day, we were focused on learning. By the time we got to skills certification, we were extremely exhausted. Our mission was to take the ladder off the truck and raise it up to a third floor burn tower. The 35-foot-ladder requires one person on each side (referred to as the Tip Person) and one person at the bottom of the ladder in back who is responsible for standing on the bottom rung and pulling with both hands with all their might as the ladder is raised. After the ladder is raised, the firefighter grabs a rope, called a halyard, and stabilizes the ladder by placing his right shoulder, hip, and the outside of the right foot against the beam. The halyard is an important part of the ladder rigging system, which is pulled to extend each section and get the ladder to the desired height. That day I was on the halyard, and the other two guys were on each side bracing the ladder while it goes up. The instructors made sure we knew the last thing anyone wants is to drop this ladder. Of course, no one wants to be that guy.

Skills test day was windy, and the three of us working the thirty-five-foot ladder had extended it three sections to its full length, and the ladder started to wobble. It began to stair-step side by side, and I heard one of my team members say, *It's going. Watch out.* Both of the other guys who were bracing the ladder on each side let go, but I didn't because I wasn't going to be that guy who couldn't handle a ladder. We had it up to the third floor of the burn tower, and as the three sections started to collapse, I kept my foot on the bottom rung with my hands on each side of the rungs, trying to brace it by myself. The dogs, which secure each section by locking it into place, were not locked and each section started coming down very fast. My team members abandoned ship, and there I stood, holding the ladder up all alone. Borrowing a phrase from a Bob Dylan and Tom Petty song, I was one guy attempting the job of three people trying to stabilize thirty-five feet of metal *blowing in the wind. How many times can a man turn his head and pretend that he just doesn't see?*

I saw very clearly that it was an impossible task because the ladder dogs were not locked in, and as I let the rope go, I braced the ladder on both sides with my hands so that it didn't fall. All of the rungs started coming down like an accordion. It was toppling pretty fast, and I realized if I wanted to keep my hands and fingers on my body, I better move them immediately! My foot was still bracing the bottom rung of the ladder and, keep in mind I'm not a six-foot three-hundred-pound muscleman. I'm fast, strong, and agile, but this ladder is a beast; and somehow, I managed to hold it up until I couldn't. When each fly section came down, the one before it hit so hard that it mashed my foot which had become entangled in the rungs.

I was in serious pain as a Recruit Training Officer (RTO), and my crew members rushed over and grabbed hold of the ladder. I stood there still holding that darn ladder with one foot while the other foot is entwined in the rungs. They were able to raise the ladder enough to untangle my foot and pull it out. It felt like the entire academy had surrounded me, and no one could believe what had just happened. Ultimately, they sent me to the hospital, where X-rays showed nothing was broken thanks to my fire department bunkers boots which had a reinforced toe box. So I had no broken bones. I had to wedge my foot out of the boot because the metal in the toe of my boot had collapsed. I was lucky because that kind of accident could have taken my foot off. Miraculously, there were no broken bones, and they didn't have to amputate my foot. I went back to the academy the next day and became known as the first guy who's ever kept a thirty-five-foot ladder from falling over by himself.

To say I was grateful to have my body sore but intact is an understatement. I owe it all to my instructors and teammates who jumped into action. The fire department is like family. In fact, it's an extension of my immediate family. We have each other's back one-hundred-percent. Firemen are away from our families ten days a month, 24 hours a day. During that period we shop, cook, train, enjoy downtime and run calls together. Getting along is very important and making sure you're competent in whatever skills are required for your position in the crew is a must because people's lives depend on it. I know that first-hand!

My first year as a probationary firefighter was a blur. I remember the first day at my first booter station, Phoenix Fire Station 25. Newbies are called booters because we get sent to the busiest stations and do a lot of running around while we're on probation. That's the best way to learn and hone your skills. Phoenix Fire Station 25 was known as a busy station with lots of fire and Emergency Medical Services (EMS) calls. I was so nervous the night before that I couldn't sleep. Would I fit in? Would I meet their expectations? Would the Captain like me? And so on, but at 5 a.m., my alarm went off.

I sprung out of bed, hit the shower, shaved my best shave, put on my neatly pressed blue uniform – which I had carefully placed next to my perfectly polished boots - and out the door I went. Booter firefighters are expected to arrive early to give the guys and gals on the previous shift plenty of relief time. We also have to get our equipment checked off before the next shift starts at 0800 hours. I was so eager that I got to the station almost 2 hours early. Excitement for the day to come had gotten the best of me, so I had to find a parking lot to hang out for the next hour before showing up for my first shift.

Pulling into the station, seeing the two big red fire trucks and other apparatuses in the bay was like finding that Christmas present you've wanted for so long under the tree. This was different– it wasn't a gift – it was something I had worked very hard to accomplish. I spent countless hours studying, networking, and learning everything about this job that got me here. Walking into the station with my gear in hand, I was greeted by a classmate from the academy who had just finished his shift. He showed me around and brought me up to speed on things he had done and learned the day before. I got to work immediately. I learned the truck, checked off my EMS equipment, and most importantly, made sure that my SCBA was topped off with air and was working properly. The academy had taught me that my equipment is my responsibility – if it fails or is not in a ready state and we get a fire, it could cost me my life.

Slowly the crew that I would spend the next three months with started trickling in. I introduced myself and made sure I looked everyone in the eye as respectfully as possible. I knew my reputation would help me on the job, and building it started on that first day.

Our Captain had a reputation as very knowledgeable with a get-it-done attitude. I had called and introduced myself to him a few shifts before mine, which is a good practice for a booter firefighter. He said I should come prepared to work, and that's exactly what I did. As he approached the fire truck, I knew the person coming toward me was the Captain. His pictures from past fires were hung throughout the station. My crew was known for having one of the most talented engineers on the job who would almost put the truck on two wheels racing to a fire or emergency call. My senior firefighter was very well respected also and is now a Battalion Chief for the fire department, and my Captain had been in charge of some of the most talked-about fires in the department. Before I knew it, the emergency tones went off and my journey began.

I had four rotations as a booter for a total of 12 months as a newbie firefighter. I have many great memories from that first year, as well as a few near misses. Some of the most talented firefighters molded me into becoming a great firefighter that first year, which gave me a good foundation for the next 20 years of my career.

CHAPTER 5

NEAR MISS

A FEW YEARS INTO MY FIRE CAREER, I was working at a bustling firehouse. It was known as "the night train" because we would run back-to-back calls after midnight. That station was an excellent station to get a lot of action, which helps mold a young firefighter. I hung my helmet there for almost four years.

One of our senior firefighters was a complete stud-athlete. In fact, he set out to climb Mount Everest, one of his life goals he was committed to tackling before he got too old. It seemed like every shift we were working out together, doing crazy things to prepare him for his grand adventure during the hot Phoenix summer – often over 115 degrees, which is hot enough to fry an egg on the sidewalk. Even though Mount Everest would be very cold when he climbed, we wanted to train in temperature extremes to prepare his body and mind. We put a circuit together in the bay of the station with a cardio area and weight area. We'd close it out by putting all of our gear on, including our SCBA. Masked up, breathing air from the backpack breathing apparatus, we'd do a skills course that included several kettlebell exercises—one arm dumbbell or kettlebell raises—doing three or four sets of 15 to 20 reps. That focused on getting him ready for the climb, step after step, conditioning his body for the long, repetitive step after step climb. We might also have a barbell station, doing similar exercises but with two forty-five-pound weights on the bar. We would lunge walk the entire rear of the station carrying that barbell across our back, taking a step with one foot, then lunge dropping your back knee just above the floor, which causes a bend in your front knee.

We had over half a football field of parking space where I'd do approximately thirty-five to fifty steps, then drop the barbell. Then he would pick it up and go his thirty-five to fifty steps. We probably made three or four loops in the parking lot just doing this. We also did some drills we learned from the training academy, strapping a huge tractor tire around our body with all of our gear on and do three or four lengths of the fire station. Next, we'd go to the garage area where the fire trucks, ambulance, and smaller trucks are kept, to our stair climb machine where we would simulate climbing 50 flights of stairs in timed intervals. By then, our legs and lungs were burning. In the beginning, we would have to use the SCBA sometimes to make sure we were getting enough oxygen to our muscles. When the Arizona heat was 110°F to 115°F, we scaled down the workouts to pushups and shoulder presses. Other guys joined us during the months we did this, all of us preparing his lungs, heart, muscles, and mind, but they all dropped out sooner or later. I was determined to see it through; how often could I help someone achieve a life goal? Especially something as grueling and dangerous as climbing Mount Everest. As it got closer to his climb, we increased the intensity of the workouts. Finally, when his time came to tackle this lifelong dream, he was ready – a lean, mean climbing machine.

He set out for his adventure knowing he had a specific window of time to make this happen because of conditions on the mountain. He knew climbers don't always make it to the top, and worse than that, some don't make it home. He stayed in touch as much as he could, giving us and everyone else who loved and supported him updates on how things were going. We'd cheer him on, and he was a guy who would cheer on the other climbers as they'd start to drop back. The climb is at an extremely high altitude, but the workouts and all the breathing work we did prepared him for that. We didn't see him for a month, but he did summit Mount Everest and I felt like a little of me was up there with him. He shared amazing videos and stories of his adventure when he returned. We'd all gather around the fireplace outside and listen to everything that happened during his climb for hours.

As everything started settling back into a regular routine of working together, responding to calls all night, going back to the station exhausted, and sleeping for half the next day, I was having a blast. One early morning after a night of grueling calls and being up all night, a fire tone coming through the dispatch system woke us. We jumped out of bed, threw on our clothes, and hustled to the truck to get our turnouts on to be ready to go when we got to the location. It was business as usual, or so we thought.

Pulling out of the bay, there was enough light for us to see a huge column of thick, black smoke pouring from a bright red glow into the morning sky, which means this fire was close. Almost too close, we didn't even have the time to rub the sleep out of our eyes. With my long-time partner in the back seat, we were ready to go into battle. Pulling into the street where the fire was burning hot, we had to contend with cars parked in front of the house making our access a bit more complicated. It was early enough that families likely had not started their morning routine. I knew this could be really bad. My Captain, who was nearing retirement and had 32 years on the job, turned his head, looked at both my partner and me, and said, "watch your assess. This house is a death trap."

We'd had many run-ins with this house over the years. The residents were known to do things that were usually not up to code. We had also gotten complaints about the homeowner doing things late at night causing suspicion among the neighbors. I had never set foot inside this house until that fateful morning. Pulling up to the house every firefighter knew his job and it was time to put all our training into action. I had never seen so much black smoke billowing out of a house before. It seemed everywhere I looked, something was on fire. I jumped out of the truck, threw on my SCBA, and pulled my hose line off the truck just like I've done hundreds of times before. Hustling to the front door, I thought to myself, there is no way in hell we're going in.

With the Captain confirming what I was thinking, we decided to go through the backyard and attack the fire from the unburnt portion in the back. The only problem was this house was like Fort Knox. There was a tall RV gate that we had to scale just to get into the backyard. I had magical shoes on that morning, lifted myself onto the gate, and jumped over in one fell swoop – in one jump. I impressed myself because I'm just 5'8" and felt like I just jumped over a house! It was my own" Mount Everest" moment, accomplishing the seemingly impossible. The only problem was when I landed, the whole side of the house was on fire, and I didn't have a hose. I started yelling for the line and finally saw it come over the gate and started fighting the fire right away. The side yard was filled with all sorts of junk making it extremely difficult to maneuver myself and pull the hose through. I entered what seemed to be an add-on garage that was completely engulfed in fire and continued my attempt to reach the back door. After fighting my way through the add-on structure, extinguishing fire as I advanced the line, I got to a sliding patio door and used my nozzle like a hammer to shatter the glass. I took a quick look around to see if my senior firefighter was behind me, but I was on my own at this point.

We were taught to help each other maneuver the line allowing the nozzle men to advance forward, so I assumed he was humping the hose through the steam. From being in other firefights, I assumed he would be right behind me eventually, so I went on and when I got inside, the house was a ball of fire. I was in what seemed to be the kitchen or dining area with my nozzle open all the way, attacking the fire head-on. It became incredibly dark and hot. Eventually, I was blinded by the steam and black smoke I created dousing flames with my hose. I heard the fire crackling that seemed to still be all around me and realized I had not made progress dousing the fire. I started to get a little worried and was losing my bearings even though I was making my way along a wall, and I had a good hold of my hose line.

Those are two lifelines in situations like the one I found myself in because if you stray from walls or lose your hose, you can easily get disoriented. If you have your hose you can find your way out. I also like to close my eyes and avoid any visual stimulation that could distract me as long as I have my hose in hand. Eyes closed also sharpens your other senses, and I heard a loud crack from above my head. Something came crashing down on me and I was knocked unconscious. I don't know how long I was out or what exactly happened. All I knew is that I was burning up when I awoke and didn't have my hose line and thought, *this is it, I may not make it out of here.* I heard my partner yelling for me, but there was no way I would make it to him. My Personal Alert Safety System (PASS) alarm, an emergency sounding alarm attached to the SCBA and activated when a firefighter remains motionless for approximately 15-30 seconds, was going off because I had been down for at least 30 seconds, probably much longer. And my low air alarm was sounding off, warning me to get out. I tried to stand up, but it was too hot and my ears started to burn, but I could hear my radio; *Larson, come in, firefighter Larson, where are you, what's your location.*

I couldn't pay attention to that because I heard what I thought was my line whipping back and forth. I must've gotten knocked out, and my hose was still on. I started reaching up into the black smoke, waving my hands as they were burning, frantically trying to grab the line. Luckily, the line hit me in the leg from the erratic movement it was making, so I tracked down the nozzle, grabbed it, and started to get back in the firefight, ultimately trying to find my way out. I remember feeling a wall, like they teach you in the academy, and rubbing my hand along it, hoping to find a window or a way out. With almost no more air left in my SCBA tank the mask was sucking up to my face. I had very little energy left when I felt a slight indention in the wall – it was a window!

Somehow, probably a rush of adrenaline, I broke the window, raised myself up, and heaved myself out. I landed on some rocks and started throwing all my gear off as quickly as possible because I was burning up. Ripping off my mask, I remember another crew member running up and spraying me with water to cool me down. My turnouts were melted, my hands were burned, and my ears were sluffing off. They dragged me to the awaiting ambulance, which is always on the scene because we're dispatched as one unit on fires.

I remember being so thankful to be alive. Not many people know what it feels like to be in a firefight and feel like you're going to succumb to it. I did, and I never want to experience a situation like this again – it is terrifying!

Out of everything that hurt, the thing that stood out was my neck. I could barely move it. It felt like I was hit by a car. We later found out what fell on me was a small air conditioning unit that crashed down from the roof and knocked me silly. I met up with my crew, who all gathered around me making sure that I was ok. It was good to see everyone else was ok as well. I was transported to the hospital and was off for a couple of months rehabbing my injuries, especially my neck. I recovered and went back to the daily grind of the job soon enough. It felt really good to be back.

The natural progression in the fire department is to promote and advance within the ranks. Several of my fellow firefighters and other colleagues began telling me that I should start studying for the Captain's position, saying I would probably be promoted. I thought long and hard about what direction I wanted to take in my career. I had accomplished my dream of becoming a firefighter, but am the type of person who questions what else I can do. What can I become in this life? Many firefighters have side jobs since we only work about ten days a month, twenty-four hours at a time. In the Phoenix metro area, we're always very busy. People often ask me what firefighters do during that twenty-four-hour period when we're not running calls. Our lives in the fire department are just like in your home environment. We come in and check off all of our gear and equipment, including our EMS equipment, for when someone is having a life-threatening medical emergency. We also check off all of our equipment on the different trucks and the truck itself. And, of course, catch up on each other's lives. You see, the station crew is my second family. We spend almost the same amount of time together as we do with our real family in the home atmosphere of the fire station. We work out together, shop, cook, and eat together. Heck, we even sleep in close quarters together. So it's inevitable that we become like family. We talk about each other's lives, partake in big life events, and develop that tight bond. But most of our days, we serve those who need our help. We show up for people on what could be one of the worst days of their life. Our job is to be prepared at any time, day or night. During downtimes between calls, we all have our own thing going on. Some of us catch up on projects, movies, workouts, or just on ways we can work better as a crew. I've always been someone who likes to push myself. I like to be uncomfortable, meaning, if I'm comfortable, I feel complacent. I'm very driven, and when I want something, I'll work harder than anyone else to get what I want. A passion of mine has always been investing, but I didn't know anything about it. One of my favorite movies growing up was Wall Street, where I first learned about investing money. I always wondered if I could do something like the guys in that movie. Once something is in my head, it sticks with me, but life has funny ways of sometimes deviating from your dreams.

photo: Mia visits Pappa at work

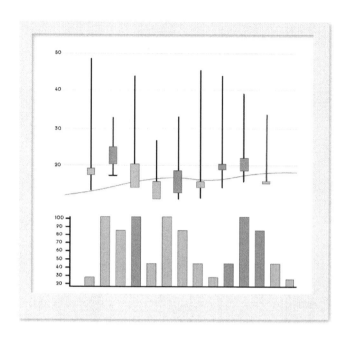

CHAPTER 6

TRADING LIFE

LOOKING BACK AT MY JOURNEY, I think a few moments really solidified and justified what I wanted to do with the second half of my life. Having worked for the fire department for over twenty years, I knew community service was important to me, but I didn't know in what capacity. As it turns out, where I am and what I'm doing today is a blessing to my wife Kate and me. I love what I get to do every day.

I'll tell you where all this started. It was just an ordinary day, and after a long hard shift I came home, laid down, turned on the T.V., and began browsing channels stopping on CNBC. For some reason, I watched all the stock data at the bottom of the screen. I listened to what the commentators were saying: ... *the 1-year chart of Apple... the fifty-day moving average... the S&P 500... the support and resistance of the index.* But, I thought, *what the heck is an index, and what in the world are they talking about?*

I wasn't a great student, as you know, but my quest to pass the fire department tests taught me a lot – or so I thought. I had no idea what was ahead of me because of this new interest in trading and knew I had to consider my options. You remember my parents' wish that I just graduate from high school and get my diploma. So that became my goal in high school. Back then, I was an athlete and hung around with a fun group of friends – jocks and cheerleaders mostly – and now I'm a firefighter. Laying there thinking about my future after a grueling shift at the firehouse, I soon dozed off. I dreamed about my favorite movie, but I was the guy on the trading floor in the 1987 blockbuster *Wall Street,* which reminded me of another film I've always enjoyed, *Trading Places.* So after my short nap and spending a minute or two getting that dream out of my head, I got up and continued the day's chores which were my nightly routine. I was eager to clean up the house because my girlfriend, who is now my wife, was coming home.

We didn't have a cook at the station, so in between our chores and whatever calls we got, there was a lot of time to learn how to put together a good meal and a hungry group of firefighters ready to eat it. We firefighters get a lot of practice cooking, and I prepared a delicious meal for my girlfriend and me. I don't exactly remember what we had, but I'm sure we both enjoyed it. We sat down to relax and watch T.V. after dinner, flipped through the channels, and *Wall St.*, a movie I could gladly watch a hundred times, came on. *No way! Is this a sign?* I thought to myself since I'd been dreaming about the stock exchange trading floor that very afternoon. In bed that night, I couldn't help but wonder if I was meant to become something more than just a firefighter. I've seen hundreds of firefighters that I respect tremendously come and go from this job. The more I lay there. I couldn't imagine being something else – redefining myself one more time. But the weird coincidence of that evening stayed with me.

A couple of days later, I went to the bookstore and picked out some educational books on investing. As I said before, I've always had an interest in investing but never pursued it. I knew that people who did that kind of work were college graduates with degrees in finance or something similar. Given my difficulty with school and testing, I never thought I could learn enough to make it in that business, but this time it was different. I felt up for a challenge. I was different, and the circumstances were different. Firefighters have a couple of retirement accounts we can put our money into through the fire department, which can be managed by a third party specializing in public safety workers.

The guy who kept our accounts had been a firefighter but retired and started a financial practice because of an unexpected accident, which I thought was amazing. He met with me every year and reviewed my accounts, and it felt like I was getting sound advice, so I was happy enough about my savings. Then, one day I happened to hear an ad on the radio while driving which had a call to action *"if you've ever dreamed of being a trader, give us a call."* My blood rushed through my body hearing that, so I pulled over, wrote the number down, and immediately called. It was a trading school not too far from where I lived, and they offered a free two-hour class on trading, which I scheduled for the following week. I was excited and skeptical, all at the same time, and couldn't help but think – *there's a catch. I just don't know what it is.* I could not believe a school was so close to me, teaching regular people how to make money from trading! *Why haven't I heard about it before?*

When my scheduled class day finally arrived, my heart was pounding, and my hands were sweaty, just like my first day as a firefighter. I was excited to get started! I wanted to challenge myself once again and set a goal outside my comfort zone, and at the end of the two-hour session, I was convinced that I had found my next calling. The teacher presented a few classes that the school offered where students could pick which asset class they'd like to learn about next. After discussing a few of the options with one of the instructors, I signed up for a 5-week foreign exchange (Forex) trading class. Forex is all about foreign currencies, so I would be learning about the Japanese Yen and what makes it strong or weak against the U.S. Dollar, for example. It sounded kind of sexy to me and was something that I had never really considered before, and told my wife, Kate, about it when I got home. She's been supportive and encouraging about my interest in trading, which was crucial to my decision to continue in the program and learn as much as possible.

I fell in love with my wife the first time I saw her, which has to be the smartest thing that I have done so far in my life. Kate is a wonderful girl who loves life. I met her at a bar the night she and her girlfriend Katie were there to celebrate their friend Carrie's birthday. That was back in 2003. Believe it or not, the girl I dated before meeting Kate actually pulled a gun on me once; it was a pretty toxic relationship from the beginning. I met her while attending some fire science courses through the community college. She was trying to get hired with a fire department like I was. We hit it off at first, but we grew apart. When I finally tried to close this chapter of my life, it escalated pretty fast. The next thing I remember, I had a gun at point-blank range to my chest. The experience with that girlfriend forced me to examine my life choices carefully. It's true that our biggest mistakes become our greatest teachers. Unlike me, my wife took her college studies very seriously and vowed not to get into a serious relationship while she was in school. Kate was born in the Philippines, came to the United States with her mom when she was six years old and is the first college graduate in her family. Her education was very important to her, so the night we met, Kate kept pushing her friend Katie toward me, wanting me to ask her friend on a date. I remember thinking that Kate was gorgeous and hoped she felt I wasn't too bad looking. Kate told me later she did think I was cute, and when I told her I was a firefighter, she caved. I could tell she softened a little because we met two years after the Twin Towers bombing when the world watched firefighters and other first responders stepping up to save lives in treacherous situations, but I wasn't using that as a come-on. I knew that night when I saw her there was something special about Kate. In fact, I was still living at my parent's house at that time, and when I came home that night, I told my mom about meeting this beautiful girl that I was going to marry.

Of course, Mom didn't believe me. Though we moved in together shortly after we met, it took about seven years for us to finally get married after planning an elaborate wedding, which never happened. Because of that, Kate's family lost trust in me. I had a phobia about marriage because so many first responders I know get divorced, and I was terrified about the church wedding that Kate's family wanted for us. Kate understood, but nobody else did. I had to earn back the trust of Kate's big family and work on my own issues, but I did, and we had a beautiful wedding. Kate is my stalwart supporter, no matter how good or bad my ideas are. She was there for me one-hundred-percent when I brought up the idea of getting into trading. I knew the night I met her that she was the one for me, and now we have a beautiful, energetic daughter named Mia and an infant son named Bryson. I never thought I would have a family of my own. I'm grateful beyond words for my daughter, who calls me Papa and is full of energy just like I was, and a son that I'll play ball with and teach so many things one day. Kate and I built this business for our family and all of the families we serve. Now more than ever, we realize how important financial security is.

Photo: Ryan, Kate, Mia, and Bryson at Papago Park right where it all started, in Tempe. Photo Credit: Kaelin Shaker

I learned everything I could about Forex for the next five weeks with Kate's complete and unwavering support. The first week was all about having the right mindset, which is a different mindset than firefighting. We're focused on assessing a situation quickly and taking action based on the skills, equipment, and team we've learned about and trained with. As traders in the market, what we have to master is a rule-based approach. That means learning about the rules and laws that govern trading, learning about market trends, how current events worldwide influence them, and so much more. Both of my jobs require a service mindset, but I also had to conquer my fear of books, numbers, and test-taking. I had to force myself to sit down, study, and use my brain more than my body. I was committed to learning the rule-based approach, understanding things like entry and exit points, and never being surprised by a trade. The course taught how to chart market activity using a "candlestick," a chart where you record market activity daily and watch the peaks and valleys, which are the candlesticks. These charts are never a smooth line with all of the markets' ups and downs, so I learned to look for trends over time by seeing patterns created over several months or years. When you read a chart, trending up it's called green (go) which means the investment is profitable, and trending down is called red (stop), meaning unprofitable. By analyzing the candlestick when trading and seeing risk potential, I learned to use a stop-loss order. If a trade goes down, it hits my stop limit, and I can move on to the next trade. I also learned about risk/reward trade-off and how to decide when to risk a dollar to make a 3:1 or 5:1 return on my money.

The second week was an introduction to the markets, but I had no background in finance and didn't understand anything about the economy. I had a big learning curve ahead of me and knew I had to do whatever it took to grasp what was coming! We started learning about unemployment, G.D.P., Non-farm payroll, and the claims report, which summarizes all unemployment claims in the country for a given period. These topics are only a fraction of what can affect the markets, and we had to learn about all of these concepts for every country that's traded on U.S. Forex markets. I spent hours and hours studying charts in the same way that I prepared for the fire exam. It takes repetition to learn anything you want to master. What I was learning was to understand and someday master the market and market trends.

The third week is when things started to get really interesting for me. The instructor began teaching us about technical analysis, and I was already excited about what I was doing. My eyes lit up when they opened their charting software, silly as that may sound. I thought *this is going to be fun!* We started to learn basic terminology like supply/demand zones, support and resistance lines, trend lines, and moving average. We had fantastic instructors who had been doing this for a very long time and marked up the charts they showed us so quickly that I couldn't keep up. They fast-forwarded charts and showed us when the investment bounced, meaning it hit a new high. We went through these fundamentals repeatedly then started to layer different metrics to increase the probability of success on a trade. I would stay after class and talk to the instructors about what they did in certain situations. I picked their brains as much as possible and learned about software that charted data from 1980 through 2000, which I bought. It allowed me to run all the charts I needed and see month after month or year after year on any investment I was interested in buying. I could see if an investment would drop or bounce, which means it hits a certain value high-point and goes past it.

On week four, we set up practice accounts with fake money and processed trades. The instructors would talk us through the different kinds of trade orders and why one made sense versus the other in certain situations. We would go through a perfect setup for eight hours a day and watched candlesticks bounce around for hours and hours. Eventually, we began to hypothesize where the next candle would start and if it would be a green *bull* or red *bear* candle. We predicted the relative strength of each trade and what direction the trend would take.

On the fifth week, the school put real dollars into our accounts. I can tell you now that paper trading and live trading are completely different worlds. You would think the trading mindset would stay the same because I was using what I just learned and practiced, but the fact that it's an actual transaction with someone else's money made me feel extreme responsibility for that trade. I quickly realized why everything we were taught in the first week was so necessary. Risk management of any transaction is the number one thing that determines a successful trade vs. one that will lose a person's money. I would be lying if I said I was a good trader on week five of the five-week course – I was horrible and blew up multiple accounts. But, like anything else, a successful trader learns from their mistakes. After graduation, some traders go home, put $100k into an account, and blow through that money in a week.

Being a firefighter, I didn't have $100k to throw into the market. I was very disciplined after understanding what I did wrong and what I needed to improve on. I decided to open a demo account and sat for hours on my days off, watching the natural progression of the charts from years back. I started focusing on each candle and what price it would be from that point forward. Studying charts became an obsession for me. I would start each day at 2 am when specific markets were open and overlapping and watch key news announcements to see what they did to the price. For example, when non-farm payroll hit, I noticed that it coincided with the markets. So if it came back positive, the markets would sometimes move up. If it was negative, the markets would move down. Non-farm payroll is the opposite of unemployment, and it measures the number of U.S. workers, excluding farm workers and other job classifications. I used this metric as a layering system to increase my trade probability.

After a year or so, I got into a rhythm and funded an account with around $500, so I could place trades based on my risk/reward metrics and what the charts were telling me. I would put in my order, go to work, and forget about it, not wanting to micromanage my trades. I learned from previous experience that if I sat there micromanaging a trade when it started to go against me, all of my rules went out the window. I would change the order and do something that might hurt my trade rather than help it. I eventually saw more winners than losers, which was a great feeling, and started making money in the Forex markets. Things were finally going well, or at least I thought. Kate and I were living in our dream condo, which I discuss in the next chapter, but the dream quickly turned into a nightmare.

CHAPTER 7

SINKING SHIP

LOOKING BACK, I WISH I knew then what I know now. During this time, the market – which means stocks, bonds, and commodities – was strong, and my trades were making money, earning about a three to one risk ratio on each trade. I had no kids yet, so I'd get up very early in the morning and catch up on world news before charting any stocks.

The way I looked at current events around the world and here in the U.S., along with charts and other data improved, and so did my ability to decide whether or not to place an order. It's important to realize that trading is a lot like placing a bet. There is always risk involved, so investors have to do all the necessary due diligence to understand the odds for and against the transaction being considered. The other thing going for me at that time was that I still had a very stable job as a firefighter with a regular paycheck.

I wanted to invest in a high-rise development in Tempe, Arizona, along Tempe Town Lake, where I grew up. At the time, I was living in Gilbert and thought the condo would be a great investment property. Tempe Town Lake, which I talked about a little in Chapter 1, improved the town's economy, so my old neighborhood was very different than when we kids played in the dry riverbed behind our house. The Tempe Town Lake condos started at around $600,000 and got incrementally more expensive on the higher floors with more expansive views. Kate and I looked at a condo with about two thousand square feet near a great path overlooking Tempe Town Lake and Tempe Butte, which locals call A Mountain because of the 60-foot-tall gold-painted letter 'A' near the top, which represents Arizona State University. A Mountain is one of my favorite places to hike, watch the sunset, and sometimes process my thoughts and clear my head. I wanted a condo on the 4th floor with a price tag of about $800,000 before hitting the design studio. Feeling somewhat comfortable with the investment but not wanting to overleverage myself, I decided to ask my brother if he was interested in investing in the property as a co-investor. Rob was doing very well in real estate at the time, so after talking things out, looking at the condo and all the numbers, he felt comfortable investing in the property. I love my brother and wanted us to be together in this venture. I thought it would bring us closer. My brother Rob and my family are the most important people in my life, and this felt right.

The high-rise property, called Bridgeview at Hayden Ferry Lakeside, was a 12-story development with all the amenities of a New York City condo. The complex would be under construction for two more years when we invested and would eventually have a private gym, pool, sauna, and game room when completed. When Kate, Rob, and I finally moved in January of 2008, the economy was still strong, and people were buying houses. The strong market was rocking and rolling with the Dow and S&P breaking records, but everything began losing steam in a blink of an eye. Some months into 2008, the market was facing a housing crash. By September 29th of that year, the Dow Jones Industrial Average fell 777.68 points, the largest point drop in history. The stock market crash of 2020 holds the biggest decline in history record now, but in 2008 I convinced my brother to take a substantial financial risk. Rob and I purchased the condo well before the housing crisis, but it took two years to complete the twelve-story building. We invested big money back then in what turned out to be a horrible investment. During those two years, people started losing their jobs and their homes. My brother and I had safe, stable employment and knew we just had to sit tight and ride out the storm. But when our condo's value dropped from about $1 million to $400,000, fear and concern about our overall financial wellbeing took over. The market crash blindsided us, and we had to rethink our strategy.

We worked as hard as possible for the next two years to keep the paychecks rolling in and were on time with every mortgage payment until it felt like a losing battle. Completely upside down on the property, our mortgage was more than twice the condo's value, and it no longer made sense to stay. It felt like we were burning our hard-earned dollars even before we earned them! After living in that home for two years, we made the difficult decision to foreclose on the 4th floor Bridgeview at Hayden Ferry Lakeside luxury condominium – the investment we had planned to own for two years and sell at a nice profit. My brother went back to living in his rental house in Mesa, Arizona. I was fortunate to have finally married Kate about a year before all of this happened after working extremely hard to earn her entire family's trust.

I told you about the big wedding that never happened. All of Kate's relatives in the Philippines made arrangements to be in Arizona for the wedding. Many tears were shed when we told both sets of parents. Kate and I probably cried the most, but the decision to postpone the wedding was mutual. We had to tell our extended family and closest friends who were coming to celebrate with us that it wasn't happening, and they were angry! Thankfully, we had not sent out the 200 invitations to extended family and friends yet, but the word got out about what happened. Kate's family near and far did not trust me, but Kate understood my fears and helped me understand them, too. She says I was "excommunicated" from her family, and it took a little while for me to regain their trust. During that time, Kate's love and loyalty never wavered. She says my eyes speak to her, and I am so glad they do because we lost a good deal of money from that big wedding that never happened. We had paid several deposits that we didn't get back, but we gave ourselves a year to move past the fiasco. In the end, we decided to elope to Kauai to get married and have a small wedding with only our immediate families and a few very close friends. It was one of the best decisions we've made. My new wife and I hosted a wedding reception at the condo when we got back. That party was our last memory-making event at the 4th-floor luxury condo.

Kate's upbringing was much different from mine. Her parents taught her to be responsible, loving, and loyal. She was a good student and a very hard worker, and when it came to money, her parents taught her that money doesn't come easy and that you have to work for it. She told me that her parents cut her off right when she got her first job as a senior in high school. Right then, her parents took that opportunity to teach her the value of money, the importance of saving, and having good credit. Basically, she never received any handouts from her parents. What they gave her, which I want to provide for my children, was a college education, free of student loans. So, when the condo investment didn't pan out, we were able to rely on Kate alone to purchase our next house in Scottsdale. The place was outdated but had great bones, so I spent about six months remodeling it, which I think was therapeutic for me. We ended up living there for over ten years. Remodeling the house gave me something new and positive to focus on – we raised the ceiling, removed walls, and uprooted old piping. We didn't spare any expense on this house, knowing we would be living there for the foreseeable future. For the next few years, I worked as much overtime at the fire station as I could. The foreclosure left me in a nasty financial hole, so I put trading on hold. I couldn't risk losing any money in the stock market because I was broke from our two disasters, the canceled wedding and foreclosure. I also decided to move away from my financial adviser through the fire department because I saw no progress; there was no growth in my retirement accounts. Kate's parents worked with an adviser that they and Kate were happy with, so she and I met with him to go over our financial situation.

After some discussion, we decided to move forward with him and transferred my retirement accounts to his firm. I still had a passion for trading but was scared of the market after investing almost $200,000 of my own money into the condo and losing it all. The new adviser was great, and every year, he met with Kate and me. He was a middle-aged man who owned a small firm. His two daughters worked for him, and his wife came in to help now and then. It seemed like a very efficient business, and we quickly built a relationship, occasionally discussing details from my trading days. I showed him the trades that I made over the years, he was very impressed, and it wasn't long before he asked if I would like to join his firm. I was taken aback because what he did was completely different than Forex, which I was used to. His business primarily worked with pre-retirees and retirees, focusing on financial planning to ensure that people had enough money to live out their dreams in retirement. I researched his business because I wanted to get back into trading and thought learning what he did for his clients would help me become a more well-rounded investor.

Before joining the business and legally work in that office, I had to take a few Financial Industry Regulatory Authority (FINRA) General Securities Representative Qualification Exams. I was required to have two licenses called Series 7 and Series 66. The Series 7 exam is focused more on stocks, bonds, mutual funds, and options, which were right up my alley. I remember in the movie *Wall Street* Charlie Sheen had to pass the same test. The other test, called Series 66, is focused on state suitability requirements to stay compliant when working with clients. Getting this job meant I had to focus on testing, which required hours of studying, just like when I had my eyes set on employment with the fire department. I discussed our investment adviser's job offer, the required exams I'd have to pass, and the hours of study ahead of me with my wife. Once again, Kate did not hesitate one second before saying, "Go for it, Ryan."

I hurried over the next day to let our adviser know that I was on board, Kate was too, and I would very much like to work with and learn from him. To take the Series 7 and Series 66 exams, I had to be associated with and sponsored by a FINRA professional. He eagerly sponsored me, but I had to purchase all the study material and courses myself. I signed up for an intense learning program through a school that I found and received my study materials a few days later. I was intimidated when I received a book of about 700 pages, with a table of contents full of subjects that I had never heard of. I also got a study guide and workbook that were helpful to my understanding of the concepts in each chapter. I studied for about six months, usually setting up study times at the library on my days off. My routine became putting in about 1ten hours of studying every day. I would go to the fire station, do my check off on the truck, check in with the crew to catch up on life, then after an hour or so, break away from the others and hit the books. It was exhausting the first six months, running fifteen to eighteen calls per shift, along with shopping, cooking, and cleaning, then I'd try to put in ten more hours studying. There were many late nights, but I was committed to see this through and get my FINRA credentials.

The Series 7 test was seven hours long with two fifteen-minute breaks and approximately two hundred and fifty questions – it was a beast of a test! While researching which course to take, I read about people failing the Series 7 time after time. It struck me that lots of these individuals who did not pass the tests graduated from college with flying colors and were already employed in some aspect of the financial industry. I found chat rooms online where people talked about failing the Series 7 test after graduating from Ivy League colleges. I thought, *what did I get myself into!* Just to graduate from high school, I struggled and had to work hard.

After six months of studying and completing a week-long course to prep for the exam, I was ready to take the test. Students have three opportunities to take the seven-hour test and need a 75% or better to pass. I scheduled the test date and was in cram mode until test day, and needless to say, I couldn't sleep the night before. The testing facility consisted of a room full of cubicles with headphones and a computer. The testing process was very strict and under the watchful eye of a proctor who walked up and down the room, observing everyone and everything we did. Test-takers were verified through their driver's license and were provided two pieces of scratch paper for the math section. I want to back up just a little and remind you that I was never a great test taker, so this was a huge deal for me. During grades K- 12, I was a below-average student and never really applied myself in school. My parents were ecstatic that I got passing grades and graduated from high school, but what I've learned about myself over the years is that if I apply myself, I can learn anything.

Applying myself, diligently studying long hours every day, doing the coursework, and completing the workbook is exactly what I did for the Series 7 test. It was similar to the effort I put into studying for the fire department exams. I knew the challenges of getting a job with any fire department in Arizona. Out of approximately 1,500-2,000 candidates, after two or three failed tests, my results were top of the list, and I was offered the Phoenix Fire Department job. Fire Department exams don't rely only on a written score. The reality of these comprehensive qualifying exams is that you're scored on a written exam covering topics like mathematical reasoning, which I struggled with all through school, mechanical reasoning, reading comprehension, spatial orientation, situational judgment, observation, and memory. They also check your personality to make sure you are up to the pressures of the job. Not only that, there's a physical component that tests strength, endurance, balance, agility, and more, all while candidates wear fifty-pound gear.

Once through that, there are two to three oral board interviews because firefighters interact with public officials and ordinary citizens frequently, so you've got to think fast on your feet and get your point across verbally. I found myself facing the same type of intense testing when it came to the Series 7 test, without the physical and oral parts. I knew what I went through to pass the fire department exams. Earning my place in the world of firefighting was an uphill battle, challenging on so many levels just like my life had been, but when I put my mind to something, nothing can stop me. I learned something from each failed test and found myself getting better and better in my prep work and practice exams. That's what life is all about – setting goals, then trying, failing, learning, and growing as you achieve that goal. After about three years of testing, I was offered a position in both the Chandler Fire Department and Phoenix Fire Department. I planned to have the same kind of success with this new goal and these new tests.

Walking up to the cubicle where I would be sitting for the next seven hours during the Series 7 exam was nerve-wracking. I hoped to feel comfortable with what I was being tested on when I settled into the cubicle, but that was not the case. Everything on the page was utterly foreign to me. It was like I didn't study at all. *How can this be?* I thought. All those hours studying and dedicating myself to the process seemed like they weren't paying off! When I finished, I knew what to expect and with one click, **FAILED** appeared on the computer screen. I was devastated and walked out of the testing center, exhausted and defeated. I had FAILED! I called my wife from my car, told her the bad news, and said I would not be home right away. I needed to go to the place I called home in Tempe, hike A Mountain to look at the condo, and let that inspire me to test again. However, I had to wait two weeks to re-test and had to tell my sponsor, the adviser who believed in me. I felt horrible when I saw him, but he told me not to worry about it because only a few people pass their first time taking the Series 7. He also said most people never retake the exam because it's too much for them. Putting in the work to fill in the knowledge gaps is the differentiator if you want to succeed. With positive words of encouragement from my mentor, I walked away with my head up and went home.

That night, Kate made a delicious meal that we enjoyed, along with a few drinks, and relaxed. My wife is an incredible listener and knows just the right words to say to put me at ease. Growing up in the Philippines, her family didn't have much, and as a little girl, she played in dump yards where people throw garbage. Her philosophy is that we should be grateful for what we have and the great country we live in, filled with opportunities. She told me that I could achieve anything I want, and she would be there every step of the way. Her attitude is precisely the reason why she is such a positive influence in my life.

CHAPTER 8

IF AT FIRST YOU DON'T SUCCEED

THE NEXT DAY I WOKE RENEWED, full of life, and with a sense of what I needed to do – get back into the books! This time I vowed to put fifteen hours per day into studying as often as I possibly could. Maybe I hadn't reviewed enough before that first exam, knowing that I would be better prepared if I had. After that first test, I wrote down all the questions I could remember, pulled out the study book, and highlighted them. I also attended a live class designed to help students be fully prepared for the test. Taking that class was an excellent decision because the instructor was very knowledgeable about the securities industry and how the test was put together. We skipped to the most important chapters in the study book, which contained the bulk of the questions on the test. The class was eight hours a day for two weeks, and on the second week, I felt more confident than ever in my understanding of the concepts in the Series 7 exam. I scheduled myself to take the next available test immediately after the class was over.

In the blink of an eye, I was pulling up to the building, once again, where I would be taking the test. My stomach was in knots just thinking about what was riding on my passing this test. Approaching check in, I knew the drill, just like at the airport. With my driver's license in hand and the ticket showing my assigned testing date and time ready to give to the receptionist, I was ready! While waiting about twenty minutes for my computer to be set up for the test, I visualized staying relaxed and confident while answering each question. I was finally escorted to my cubicle and given two blank sheets of paper. I filled in the requested information, and off I went. Just a few hours into the test, I felt a lot more confident than on my first attempt and knew the class I attended was the reason. During the fifteen-minute break, I refreshed myself with a snack, a cold drink, and the necessary visit to the restroom. As the test progressed, closer to the end, I became very anxious and started getting a little fidgety. *Stay focused,* I told myself, but as I got to the last question, I felt a familiar mix of excitement and nerves. I knew that I could be off to a new career path with a few more clicks of the button, and just like that, I closed the test and waited for my results. It's funny, sitting there waiting for a computer to tell you your future. Before long, a screen popped up that said view results. I sat there for a minute or two, took a deep breath, and said a small prayer. I felt my blood thumping through my body and could almost hear my heart beating when I finally told myself *Here we go* and clicked "view results." Scared of what I might see, though I felt good about the test this time, I put my head down for a second before lifting it to read FAILED. I was crushed and could not believe what was staring me in the face! I felt so good about this test. I knew I had to be close to that passing grade. The words *what happened?* kept running through my mind, but I couldn't let that get the best of me.

I gathered my belongings and my pride, then walked out where the receptionist handed me my results. I looked them over carefully, realizing that I missed getting 75% by <u>one</u> question. Just one question! If you thought I was sad the first time I didn't pass, you'd be correct. This time, my sense of failure was even worse. *How could I miss it by one question,* I asked myself over and over. That was a devastating day that would play in my head for three months. Because I didn't pass on the second try, I had to wait a full three months before retaking the Series 7 and didn't know if I would be able to stay motivated and continue studying for another three months. Waiting a couple of weeks is manageable, but three months was a hard pill to swallow. I took about a week off from studying. I had gotten completely burned out from ten then fifteen hours of study time for many weeks before my first and second tries. Don't forget that I was doing that while still working a full-time job that is both physically and mentally demanding. Eventually, I made peace with failure, and having Kate comfort and encourage me again was incredible. She believes in me sometimes more than I believe in myself – my wife somehow knows how to make lemons out of lemonade.

I pulled out of my funk and took a whole different approach to stay motivated. On my days off from the fire station, I shadowed the adviser who was sponsoring me. Not only did shadowing him give me more insight into the business, watching him at work kept me motivated and confirmed my gut feeling that this industry was right up my alley. I could see myself doing the same thing as he did, helping people get a grip on their financial future, and that felt good. I attended all of his presentations on retirement planning over two nights at local colleges as well as attending fancy presentations we hosted at restaurants like Ruth's Chris Steak House and Flemings. My job was to give each attendee a workbook and make appointments with those interested in further discussion. Shadowing my sponsor is precisely what I needed to grow my understanding of the business. Now I not only had book knowledge, but I was also sitting in on actual appointments with prospective clients and hearing their concerns. I began to recognize common scenarios and the questions that go with them. Most of the time, people's biggest concern was running out of money, and I would sit there taking notes during the meeting. It was refreshing to take very detailed notes and dictate them into an app that transcribed everything into a report that I could pass on to my mentor. It was more like an internship that had me bouncing from the fire station to his office, to the library, and back home to eat and do it all over again the next day. The next few months flew by, and I finally scheduled my last test.

I would most likely hang it up and stop chasing the dream of becoming a licensed adviser if I didn't pass the test on try number three. Every time I had to get into the mindset of studying for Series 7, it got a little harder to study and stay motivated. Getting my FINRA credentials was something that I aspired to because being a financial adviser is about service, which I love to do. Preparing for the Series 7 test had already used up virtually all my free time for about a year at this point, putting a lot of other things in my life on hold. Don't forget that I still had another test, Series 66, to pass before I could work in our Financial Adviser's office.

Here I was for the third time, sitting in a cubical staring at the same screen which I'd already focused on for *fourteen* hours. I knew this time I *had* to earn that all-important score of 75%. I began clicking away as I read through each question thoroughly. Though the questions cover the same concepts, each test is different, so every question is new, and I couldn't just blow through it. I had to think through each one with that ever-present knot in my stomach when taking these written tests. When I was preparing for the fire department exams, reading comprehension was one of the most challenging parts for me. I practiced reading comprehension questions numerous times, teaching myself how to figure out what they were looking for in my answers.

I think everything in life helps you be better, more aware of things, and more grounded. I had to learn to control my immediate reactions that were either anger or self-doubt. Without all that practice to improve my reading comprehension, I would have failed miserably on the Series 7. As I was nearing the end of the test, I felt a bit of anxiety and tried not to think about what-ifs. But after working for almost a year to pass this test, everything came down to this moment. As I clicked on my answer to the last question, my heart started beating so fast I could feel it pulsing throughout my entire body. Sitting there, I could only think about my wife and how supportive she'd been through this whole process. I submitted the results, looked away from the screen, and held my breath. When I got the courage to look, **PASSED** jumped off the screen at me. I let out a massive sigh of relief and smiled, probably the biggest dumb smile of my life, but _I did it!_

I couldn't get out of there fast enough and ran to the car with my results in hand. I got in and immediately called Kate. She picked up, and I instantly started crying. The words _I finally passed the exam_ almost didn't come out of my mouth – the poor girl probably thought that I had blown it again, and this dream was over.

As soon as I gathered myself a little bit, I said, "Kate, I passed. Can you believe it?"

Her response was predictable. "Ryan, I had no doubt."

We talked about the test for a minute or two, and I let her know I would be calling my sponsor to let him know. My next call was to my adviser, who picked up immediately as if he was expecting my call. I think he was just as excited as I was at the possibility of bringing me on as a young, hungry adviser to support his practice.

I shared the good news with him, and he said, "Congratulations, now let's get to work on the next test."

I laughed and replied, "I'm on it!"

That evening my wife and I celebrated with dinner at our favorite place, then saw a movie. Kate deserved special treatment. She supported and encouraged me through the long hours of study, my lack of time, and all the emotion I had wrapped up in this goal – the whole way. I felt so blessed.

The Series 66 exam was my next hurdle on this new journey, and I had no time to take a breather. Series 66 was created by the North American Securities Administrators Association (N.A.S.A.A.) and tests candidates on state laws by answering one hundred questions in one hundred and fifty minutes. FINRA administers the test, and to pass, I had to get a score of 73% or better. I took a few days off before diving into the books to prepare. My preparation process for Series 66 was pretty much exactly what I did to get ready for the Series 7. I studied for the next three months before taking the exam for the first time. I had studied hard for twelve weeks and felt confident, so I scheduled the test for the following week. I had taken so many tests over the last several years that I became confident in my test-taking and ability to learn. I had proven to myself that I could accomplish anything if I applied myself, no matter what challenge.

Too bad I didn't have that mindset in high school! I was very small in stature, and my freshman year, weighing just 98 pounds, I wrestled in the 103-pound weight class that year and the 112-pound class sophomore year. I didn't hit my growth spurt until the summer before my junior year, when I shot up like a rocket. That year, I weighed 140 pounds and dropped weight to wrestle in the 125-pound class.

Finally, I weighed in at 160 pounds in my senior year and lost enough weight to wrestle at 140. My fluctuating weight is important because I didn't have much confidence when I was wrestling. Still, people around me saw something that I didn't. My coaches and teammates would always talk about my wrestling skills. There was still some doubt at times in my senior year and when that crept into my mind, I would lose confidence in myself and my mom could see it. She had a sixth sense. I was named team captain my senior year and needed to step up and lead. I knew that I had to instill confidence in myself and be the person my coach and teammates saw in me but wasn't sure how to. My mom knew me very well and could predict when I was going to lose a match. The reason? Confidence. She could sense when I didn't believe in myself and knew when my efforts would not pay off. By the end of my senior year, I had a record of 34-3 and was ranked number one in the state, but only placed third at the end of the season. I lost the last match that would have taken me to the State Championships. Why did I lose? Lack of confidence. Emotionally, I went back to my seventh grade experience in my first year of wrestling. I placed third in our region that year and made it to the State Championships but lost to a redhead in eighth grade who was bigger than me. Doing so well in seventh grade wrestling without knowing anything about the sport made me feel really good about myself – but that loss put me right back into a loser mindset – and the same thing happened my senior year. I looked at my opponent and subconsciously decided that he was better than me because he was bigger. I was placed in the loser's bracket and had to claw my way out and ultimately placed 3rd in state but that loss eliminated my chance to be a state champ. I dreamed of being a state champion, but in a blink of an eye, that was gone. I would have to fight my way back if I ever wanted a place on the podium. In the first match of the losers bracket, I was taken down numerous times. It wasn't because the other wrestler was better. I lost because I gave up. I didn't have the confidence in myself anymore.

My grandparents, who've both passed away, were always at the tournaments. They helped raise my siblings and me, as I mentioned earlier in the book. First, when my dad was in Korea, I was four, and when he was stationed in Iraq for a year during the Gulf War. He also served one year in Desert Storm when the U.S. sent troops to defend Saudi Arabia. My mom worked as hard as she could to raise four kids, not knowing if she would ever see my dad again. It was a tough time for all of us, but looking up into the stands, I remember my grandparents yelling at me to get up whenever my opponent was getting the best of me. I also remember my little sister on the rail, jumping up and down, encouraging me to stand up. I looked up at my mom with everything happening so quickly around me, and her face spoke a thousand words. She knew I didn't have the confidence to push my opponent off me and was close to defeat. I'm now the underdog' and have four years of hard work under my belt, with my loved ones cheering me on, and finally, something clicked. *This guy isn't better than me. What am I doing? Get up, Ryan. Fight.* With my coach of four years standing in the corner yelling, the one who told me to come out for the wrestling team and believe in me for so long, I stood up. I broke away from the other wrestler and attacked like there was no tomorrow, racking up twelve points in the third quarter. I went on the offensive and pinned my opponent for the win and won the next three matches finishing 3rd in the state. I won those matches because I had finally found confidence deep inside myself – at the last possible minute. From that day forward, belief in myself and my abilities stayed with me. Since that tournament in high school, I have believed in myself and know I have the confidence to do anything I set my mind to.

I reminded myself of those times while putting so much time and energy into each test. Sure, there were ups and downs during preparation and with each test I didn't pass, but confidence in myself never wavered. I knew that if I worked hard enough, I would pass the

Series 66 exam. Two hours later, when exam time was up, I closed my eyes and asked myself silently – *Did I study hard enough? Yes. Did I focus on answering each question as best I could? Yes. Was I successful?* I opened my eyes, looked at the screen, and my answer was *No*. There it was again, that dreaded word – FAILED. Even though I didn't pass, I stood up and was not feeling crushed or defeated. Instead, I felt a sense of confidence and a no-die attitude like I see in superheroes in the movies. *Ryan, you've been here before, and you can do it again*. I said to myself as I walked out of the exam room.

I was back at it again and hitting the books. The next two weeks felt like I was in the movie Groundhog Day, hoping that Punxsutawney Phil would see his shadow. Why did I continue to put myself through this? Because success is not always easy. It never has been easy for me and probably never will be. I knew that I had to hustle to get what I wanted because nothing's ever been handed to me. I've had to hit the ground running to get what I want all my life. Just like that, I found myself back at the testing site for one more attempt to pass the Series 66. *This is it – I will get 73% or better!* I told myself silently. *Believe in yourself; you can do it*. I felt that this time the answers came faster. *This is the last time*. I told myself *if you pass, you don't ever have to take another test*. This time I kept my eyes open as I clicked to see the results. **PASS,** The computer seemed to scream at me, and I was elated. I was ready to turn over a new leaf and held back tears of joy as I left the testing facility and headed home to see Kate.

A few weeks later, I received confirmation from the state and FINRA, the financial regulatory authority, stating that I could legally work at my adviser's firm. Going to work the next day as a licensed financial adviser was an easy transition since I'd already been shadowing my mentor. I was ready to hit the ground running and began doing presentations with him, which scared me to death because I was never a terrific public speaker. In high school, my voice cracked every time I had to speak in front of the class, and I still cringe in pain thinking about talking in front of a crowd. But this was my chosen field that I worked so hard for, and there was no excuse. I've never hesitated in a firefighting situation because lives depend on me. I knew that I needed to get a grip on speaking to groups of strangers because my mentor's business, staff, clients, and future clients depended on me. He wanted me to make presentations to individuals and groups interested in what our firm had to offer, and many of them had much more life experience than me. I didn't feel like a leader but realized I had to step into that role when making these presentations which requires confidence. I wasn't the best, most experienced adviser, but knew how much I learned by shadowing my mentor and preparing for all of those tests. I had proven to myself and FINRA that when I started on this journey, the world of finance and financial planning was like a foreign country where I didn't know the customs and traditions or speak the language, but I learned enough to earn the high marks required to get my licenses. If I could embrace the confidence I had on the Pop Warner field, the wrestling mat, an emergency call with Phoenix Fire, and in the FINRA exam room when talking to these clients and potential clients, I would be one of the best financial advisers out there.

I had to become a better public speaker, so I hired a coach to help me work on my craft. There is always something in life that challenges, something to master, or something new to learn. I'm in my forties now, and life has taught me that I will become stagnant if I'm not working on myself day in and day out. That's not how I was raised or shaped as a young man. Remember, the goal set for me was "just get your diploma so you can get a job." Don't get me wrong, I love my parents and know they did the best they could, but living a "just get a job" kind of life would not honor everything they did for me and my siblings, and I would not be a happy person. Luckily for me, two dreams had come true: I was still a firefighter, and my financial adviser was also now my boss, and I learned so much from him about how to run an effective practice. We often role-played in the office because there are so many things that an adviser needs to know about a client's situation before giving any recommendations. I think that's one of the best takeaways learned from my mentor. In this industry, there are salesmen, and there are advisers. Salespeople are just looking for the commission they get when selling an annuity or a life insurance policy. Understanding what I mean here is essential for anyone planning for retirement or needing a financial adviser for any reason. I will go into a bit of detail on applicable FINRA guidelines and terms a person might hear once they take that step.

CHAPTER 9

MY NEW WORLD

AN ADVISER OR A WEALTH manager looks at a person's entire financial situation and designs a plan for their long-term financial wellbeing, whether the individual is thirty-five or sixty-five. There are basically two types of financial planning business models used in the industry – the broker and the independent fiduciary. The broker, who I commonly refer to as the retail model, refers to brokers, broker-dealers, or financial planners who generally work for the big firms that we all know. Those individuals are only allowed to sell the products offered by their firm. A broker, broker-dealer, or financial planner will place your hard-earned money into a product that will suit your situation. I will go into more detail about what suitability is later on. I want readers to understand that these individuals receive a commission from each product they sell and generally work for large brokerage houses. Those big brokerage houses build all kinds of product offerings that these brokers sell. This business model has served many people for decades and has a place in the industry, without a doubt. Think of it like chain restaurants where you can only order your meal their way. If you're on a special diet, you've got to make do with what they have and hope for the best, but you still get a meal when you need it.

The second financial planning business model is an independent adviser, or fiduciary. These individuals are obligated to put the client's interest ahead of their own when recommending investments. Their goal is not to earn a commission. Instead, it is to find the right products for their clients to achieve their investment goals. Fiduciaries uphold FINRA rule 2111which says: *"A member or an associated person must have a reasonable basis to believe that a recommended transaction or investment strategy involving a security or securities is suitable for the customer, based on the information obtained through the reasonable diligence of the member or associated person to ascertain the customer's investment profile. A customer's investment profile includes, but is not limited to, the customer's age, other investments, financial situation and needs, tax status, investment objectives, investment experience, investment time horizon, liquidity needs, risk tolerance, and any other information the customer may disclose to the member or associated person in connection with such recommendation."*

Fiduciaries don't simply pull the best product from a portfolio from a shelf or drawer and say, "this is the best we have for you."

Think of this scenario as being similar to having a meal prepared by a chef who is also a nutritionist and creates a meal that tastes delicious and is full of the right blend of ingredients that contain the vitamins, minerals, fats, and other nutrients that your body needs. There is no doubt this food is the right choice for your long-term health. Fiduciary responsibility means the client's needs, based on their financial profile (Rule 2111), always come first. The adviser searches for products to create a portfolio of assets tailored explicitly for that person. An independent fiduciary can search the entire world of money to find the right product for the particular client. Advisers and brokers tied to specific brokerage houses don't have that same freedom. They have to choose from their firm's product portfolio and have a fiduciary responsibility to their client limited to the firm's offerings.

It's essential that you understand the difference between the two business models, broker and fiduciary, to ensure you get the right advice and grow a nest egg that will not let you down. On the fiduciary side, the adviser gets paid a flat fee for *assets under their*

management, which is disclosed on the investment policy statement or A.D.V. form. The A.D.V. form tells you exactly how much you are paying each year for asset management services and is a very transparent business model. My mentor would always tell me, *Ryan, do the right thing, and a client will stay a client for life.* This philosophy is what I've always believed in and stand behind. It is living the ideal: *Do unto others as you would have done unto you*, which is the reason that I'm a firefighter – I care about people.

Operating as a fiduciary is also a service-driven business model. Both my grandfather and my dad served in the military and were willing to give the ultimate sacrifice in service to this country. I didn't follow their path exactly but want to serve in a different way and be helpful to people in need. That is why I fought so hard for a career in the fire department. Firefighters and all first responders are true advocates for the community's men, women, and children. I've laid my life on the line to save others in need, as I described in Chapter 3, the 35-foot ladder incident, and Chapter 4, the house fire that landed me in the hospital. I could have lost a limb, or my life, in either of those incidents. My point is that firefighters are a band of brothers and sisters, much like our military troops. When we suit up or when we're in street clothes, our commitment is to be there for people, especially our brothers and sisters on the line, no matter where and no matter what. My mindset does not change when I'm in a business suit. I consider every client part of our family. As a financial adviser, I strive to advocate for the individuals and families I work with on their journey to a worry-free retirement.

After each presentation that my mentor and I put on, attendees scheduled time to meet and review their financial situations with us. We initially worked together in these meetings to make sure I had a good sense of what information I needed to build an effective plan for them. He had a process that we followed, and I quickly realized the importance of having a process when running a financial advising practice. Without a well-defined process, it's not uncommon that things fall through the cracks, which in the long term, could affect the client's savings portfolio. My job as an adviser deals with people's life savings – usually the money my clients worked for since a very young age. I knew that mistakes could not be made with their hard-earned dollars. So, a few years into my career, I decided to trademark a process that I had developed as I grew in knowledge and understanding of both the client and the financial landscape. I call it the Written Retirement Action Plan (W.R.A.P.) Process and describe it in more detail later in this book.

WRAP Process

Reg. No. 6,174,394	FirstLine Financial (ARIZONA LIMITED LIABILITY COMPANY) 5635 N Scottsdale Road Scottsdale, ARIZONA 85250
Registered Oct. 13, 2020	
Int. Cl.: 36	CLASS 36: Financial advisory and consultancy services, namely, the creation of personalized strategies to achieve financial independence; Financial planning consultation; Financial retirement plan consulting services
Service Mark	
Principal Register	FIRST USE 2-3-2020; IN COMMERCE 2-11-2020
	THE MARK CONSISTS OF STANDARD CHARACTERS WITHOUT CLAIM TO ANY PARTICULAR FONT STYLE, SIZE OR COLOR
	No claim is made to the exclusive right to use the following apart from the mark as shown: "PROCESS"
	SER. NO. 88-852,019, FILED 03-30-2020

Director of the United States
Patent and Trademark Office

For an entire year, I went straight to the adviser's office after working a 24-hour shift at the fire department. I often felt like Superman with two identities, though I didn't change clothes in a closet. I changed out of my fire dept uniform and into a business suit before leaving the fire station. That was an exciting time in my life that began because of my passion to recoup the enormous losses my brother Rob, Kate, and I incurred during the 2008 financial crisis. I was committed to recouping my losses from foreclosure and everything else that happened in a few short years. I began learning about the many different savings vehicles and investment tools available to me that allow my clients to have a more diversified portfolio of assets as they move forward in life. I thought studying was a thing of the past, but soon realized that my job involves continuously educating myself on the ins and outs of the many tools I would be presenting to clients throughout my career. I had a lot to do during my business suit hours. Not only was I helping new clients, I was also advising colleagues at the fire dept. At work, my brothers and sisters started to get wind of what I was doing outside of the fire station. Almost every day, someone would say, *Ryan, can you review my retirement accounts?* I started to help one, then two, soon three fellow firefighters with their 457 & 401a retirement accounts. I ended up managing almost 100 new clients in a matter of one year.

I was bringing a lot of business into the firm and started to feel taken advantage of. I was practically running the company while he was away on vacations or spending time on elaborate trips from all the new accounts I was bringing in. I started to wonder if this was what he wanted when he invited me into the company? He never said he wanted someone to come in, run the day-to-day operations, and bring in new clients paying fees with a big cut of those fees going to him. I soon learned that the answer was *yes.* That's exactly what a junior adviser is supposed to do. He was the Chief Executive Officer (CEO) of a firm that he created and was entitled to reap the benefits of my hard work. I learned everything I could about the business's day-to-day operations: what systems he had in place, the costs, overhead, and everything else. I thought to myself, *there is no way you can do this right now*, but I wasn't getting the guidance or mentorship I expected and decided I was done cutting my teeth and began thinking about how to leave the firm.

I heard about complaints from a few clients. The adviser I was working with was terminated from our broker/dealer, which required me to either follow him or seek another firm. Of course, I appreciated everything this gentleman did for me, but the writing was on the wall, and it was time for me to pack it up and find another firm where I could hang my hat. After doing my due diligence on several firms, I called an adviser who looked very promising. He was doing things that the firm I worked at did not do. One of the things that stood out to me was his building a suite of in-house portfolio of products. You recall that I had been a trader before losing my luxury condo to foreclosure and put trading on pause because I was in a different place in life. I had gambled and lost. However, trading is something I wanted to do, and I was good at it.

He accepted my call. I spoke to him for about 15 minutes, told him my story, including that I was looking to join another firm. He invited me to come in for an interview which I gladly accepted. The following week as I arrived for our appointment, I was very impressed with the aesthetic of his office. It had a great layout and a friendly secretary who immediately greeted me. I let her know I was there for an interview, and she said she'd let him know I was there. Before telling her boss that I was here, she asked if I needed anything and brought me a cold water bottle and a napkin. I thought, *wow, this is a nice touch*. Everything oozed high-end, wealth, and comfort, starting with the view, furnishings, décor, and especially the receptionist's classy service. I appreciated that. The adviser soon came out to greet me and led me into a large conference room, where we took about 15 minutes to get to know each other. I felt very comfortable knowing what I could bring to the table. There was a little bit of a pause in our conversation, and then he asked me to stand and present to him.

I was taken aback and heard myself say, *present what?* He replied, "your pitch," but I had never done this before. My other job found me, and I didn't have to pitch anything. Standing there, I didn't have a pitch and felt like a rookie student, lost in a way that's hard to explain. I'm not one to beat around the bush, so I took a leap of faith. I got up and started writing on a whiteboard in the room, educating him about my philosophies on investing. I wanted to show him my conviction and what I believed to be a sound plan if we were going to do business together. He stopped me about ten minutes into my spontaneous pitch and told me to take a seat. He then stood up, said this is how you do it, and started selling me why I should do business with him if I were a prospective client. Honestly, it felt very sales-y, and I felt like I was at a car dealership. He closed his dissertation by saying, *Now that's how you present to a prospect.* I didn't know if I was supposed to get up and clap or what, but from my research, I knew that he had a significant footprint in the industry and many connections. He talked for about another twenty minutes telling me the ins and outs of his business, then showed me around the office. He introduced me to the different departments and the people I would be working with. We concluded the interview with a handshake and him telling me he would think about it and get back to me.

I left the office confused. It wasn't a typical interview, and I felt like he was testing my communication skills to see if my way of pitching clients was like his. I went home and told Kate, who asked if I envisioned working there. What I was looking for in my career was another opportunity to learn and maximize my business expertise in order to offer something unique to my clients. Everything on the outside, the look and feel of the organization, felt great, but my gut questioned what I experienced in that conference room.

He called the next day and offered me a job. I had thought about it all night and decided there was a lot I could learn at that firm, so it was the right step to take, and I said yes. He immediately began the onboarding process, telling me that I would have my own office with a desk, phone, and computer. He added that he expected me to make calls and drum up business for the firm. I settled into my new office and kept my head down, calling soft leads from recent dinner seminars or radio ads. For two years, he was on a popular radio station in the valley on a regular basis, where he garnered a lot of business for the firm. If people called in and did not set up an appointment, my job was to reach out to them and build a relationship so they would bring their business to us. This was a very different business model than at my previous firm, and this job felt like I was simply there to make calls. I did not get much support from him and always had to search for him to ask questions if I needed guidance. His standard response was to say he was very busy, and I should make the calls and try to set appointments. A few weeks later, I saw a newly hired employee leave the company and began hearing chatter from other employees about how they were being treated. In just a few weeks, I realized there was a revolving door of new employees joining the firm as other employees were leaving it. I had a hard time keeping up with what he was doing and just kept making my calls, studying different products, and learning anything I could from this business. On one particular day when I came into the office, a lovely woman he had recently hired asked how things worked in this office. I didn't want to say not too good, which came to mind first, so I said, pretty well, hoping to form a friendship and, moving forward, help each other. She had been an analyst for a Fortune 500 company and recently moved to Arizona. She joined the firm to assist in portfolio management and grow as an adviser. We often talked when I was in the office. Hers was right next to mine, and I would pick her brain. She was a wealth of knowledge when it came to building portfolios. Much of her time was spent evaluating stocks and dissecting the financials of the business offering the stock. I looked up to her, and we had a great relationship. We've stayed connected and keep in touch regularly.

I soon began to recognize a sense of discomfort in the office, and it seemed like everyone was walking on pins and needles. After about six months with the firm, being there just didn't feel right. I couldn't convince prospective clients to enter into business with this firm, and I could not convince myself to stay either. Eventually, I handed in my resignation, shook my boss's hand, and thanked him for everything. As I collected my things and packed up, several staff members came over and asked where I was going. I wasn't sure at that point and let everyone know how helpful they were and how much I appreciated them. I kept hearing, "Ryan, you need to open your own firm. I would love to work with you someday." I was very flattered and thought that was very nice of them to say. But when two, then three, then four people said the same thing, I was shocked. I honestly felt I could start a firm and take the entire office with me since it seemed that they all wanted to follow me. I went home and began contemplating my next move.

I still had a full-time job with the fire department and didn't feel ready to run my own firm yet at this point in my career. I had a good working relationship with the current broker/dealer that I was affiliated with and a lot of my client's assets still being held under that broker/dealer's rep code. I let them know that I resigned from the firm I had been working with. They supported my decision one-hundred-percent and asked what I would like to do moving forward since I had moved from a different broker/dealer to them when joining the previous firm. I said that I wanted to keep them as my broker/dealer and preferred to look for another office in the valley to hang my hat. I needed to keep things as simple as possible and knew the amount of paperwork I'd have to prepare and process when changing a broker/dealer. The broker/dealer told me about an adviser in the north part of the valley currently affiliated with them. I thought it might be a perfect solution.

I decided to reach out to the recommended firm and see if it was a good fit. I called their office and asked to speak to the owner to see if they would be interested in meeting. The owner was a younger guy and I felt comfortable talking to him. He invited me to check out the office and said I should dress casually. Walking up to this office felt different than the first visit to my previous two firms. This office felt virtual and techie. I walked in, received a warm welcome from the receptionist, and sat down in the gorgeous lounge area. I could see that the firm had great taste. It was apparent that a lot of thought went into designing the space. The owner came out and shook my hand. Once again, I was sitting in a large conference room and, from the moment I sat down, I felt comfortable. Our conversation went well and revealed similarities between us. He asked a few questions then wanted to know about the firm I recently left. The financial planning community is somewhat of a small world, and people talk, so he knew of the firm. I shared my experience at the old firm and explained that my boss and I didn't connect. He said that he understood that sometimes people don't get along. Our conversation was going well as it was getting close to lunchtime. He invited me downstairs to continue the discussion over lunch, where we really got to know each other. I could easily see myself working with him. *So, are you ready to go?* Without any hesitation, I said *yes!*

I liked what I saw in him and what he was doing. He asked me to come back the following day to fill out the necessary forms. Working in this industry requires an agreement on revenue splits — what the company keeps and what the adviser receives. This agreement is one of the most important documents that an adviser must sign. I read through the contract carefully and felt good about the split and the terms. Once again, I was off to the races and showed up every day that I wasn't at the fire department. On those days, I put in an eight to five shift. I realized in my previous two firms that there are different business models in this industry. Some advisers are all about networking, shaking hands with powerful people, and talking about what they do. Others like getting in front of as many people as possible. These are the advisers who do a lot of dinner seminars and workshops to garner clients. Others want to be on the radio or participate in charity events. That's how the industry works, and I was currently working with a networker. The previous adviser did many radio and dinner events, and the adviser before that did workshops with some referral business. I had an opportunity to see how these very successful firms built their practices. There is no right or wrong way to create a thriving business, and each person needs to find what works best for them.

I was still somewhat new to the industry and trying to digest as much as I could. I built a pretty nice book of business because of the firefighters I was working with and never had to sell myself. I've strived to build a good reputation as a hard worker and someone easy to get along with. The first thing I learned in the fire department is that reputation is everything, and I should guard mine with my life. I have lived by that model, building trust which makes or breaks a reputation. But I never bought into the idea that my life had to revolve around the fire department 24/7. To me, life is an adventure, and once you accomplish a goal, you're on to the next one. The fire department gave me a stable platform and reliable employment for twenty years. It's the foundation for buying a home, raising a family, and putting food on the table. .I have a pension and two retirement accounts that will serve me well into my retirement years. But like any other job, if you're not pushing to be the best version of yourself, you become complacent.

I was promoted to an engineer, which means I was responsible for the fire truck a few years into my career. This gave me a new and exciting challenge from the very physical and demanding job as a firefighter where sometimes I could be in my fire turnouts for hours on end in the blistering Arizona heat on a large commercial fire. As an engineer, I'm responsible for the fire truck and all the men and women who are on board. I would be responsible for getting the necessary water at different fire incidents to the appropriate lines so that the firefighters could do their job and put the fire out. But my passion was being an engineer on a ladder. I was fortunate enough to be on some of the busiest ladder trucks in the department. An engineer on a ladder is much different than an engineer on an engine. "Ladder bucks," as they're called, get to break shit! We get to use some very cool equipment like the spreaders or jaws of life, as the media calls them, to extricate victims from motor vehicle accidents. The best part about being an engineer on a ladder truck is getting an opportunity to climb a 110-foot ladder to hang out in a bucket and spray water on a major commercial fire which I've done numerous times. It is definitely exciting to operate a ladder truck. How many kids out there think about driving a big red ladder truck? I know I had a toy ladder truck as a child. I believe there are still plenty of little kids playing with old-fashioned ones like mine or whatever modern toy fire truck is on the market today. Most of my time was geared toward fighting fires and running on EMS calls in downtown Phoenix, a very special place to be a firefighter. There are not many stations in Phoenix where you get to pull out of the bay doors, look up, and see a bunch of skyscrapers all around you. It's exciting every time! I spent almost four years at station one in downtown Phoenix. Everyone calls it the big house because it's one of the larger fire stations and is also where South deputy; a separate building that holds one Battalion Chief (BC2) and a command van (CM1) for major fire or medical emergencies, is headquartered. South Deputy is the hub where roughly 100 roving firefighters call in at approximately 0600 each morning before their shift to get their assignments for the day and what truck they would be on.

I got to see first-hand the complexity of this process unfold. South Deputy has to know something about every firefighter: where they live, where they like to work, and sometimes where they're allowed to work. This scenario is where reputation comes into play. If a firefighter doesn't fit in or get along with certain people, they will probably not do well as a rover. That's blunt but true. I was very fortunate to have the opportunity to be moved into the big house one shift and had a Captain take me under his wing. I was looking for the same thing as a young adviser because there's no better way to learn than jumping into the fire with a knowledgeable and experienced mentor. Each shift, we had to respond to something different. Like my previous assignments, we trained together, shopped together, and slept in a dormitory together. The station had two engines, one ladder, and a ladder tender: a smaller ladder truck when the large aerial ladder was not needed on a call. I bounced around from truck to truck and was kept at that station for many years because the crew liked me. Ok, I'm going to toot my own horn for a sentence or two. It is one thing to be kept roving into the same station every shift because the crew likes you enough to request you every time, but it's another thing when that station is Station 1, the big house in downtown Phoenix, and the crew is asking for you. They're the best of the best! A salty group of firefighters that have lived through it all. You name it, they've seen it. That is a big deal, and I was fortunate to be that person. I joke around that they kept me because of my impressive basketball skills even though I'm five-foot-nothing, but I'm fast. I came to really enjoy the ladder truck and the skill sets I learned to be efficient on that truck. I honestly loved the diversity of each truck. There were so many interesting characters at that station that I stayed there for about four years until I picked up a spot at Station 9, not too far away. At Station 9, I landed a permanent position as an engineer on ladder nine. Station 9 was one of those stations where everyone got along, and it seemed like we all had a common interest – the outdoors.

We planned a camping trip each year and enjoyed camping together. It was a great time to get away, connect with each other outside of work, and be one with nature. I was assigned to Station 9 for approximately four years. I grew very close with the crew because of the time we spent together. We battled many fires and had lots of fun together in our off-hours. After about four years as an engineer, I made a decision that many of my colleagues could not understand. I got used to being asked if I had lost my mind. I'd been a firefighter for about sixteen years at this point and a financial adviser for about four. I enjoyed juggling both careers. I had about a year under my belt with the current firm when I started to explore a different way to build my book of business, which is basically my clients and the value of their investments under management with me. As a new adviser, you want to hit the ground running. You are building a book of business and are in the growth phase of your career, and I decided to learn another side of the company. I was working in the investment advisory side of the industry, which is all about building portfolios for clients based on their time horizon – how long we anticipated holding an investment before the client will need to use that money – and risk tolerance. Based on their objectives, we would build out and manage that portfolio for the client. We provided them performance reporting, quarterly and annual reviews using a technology that allowed the client to view all of their assets in one place. The agreement that I signed with this firm covered assets under management. I also looked into insurance products that provided a commission based on the amount of investment in the product. I started learning about life insurance products, including annuities, finding out everything I could about those products. Some products were good, and others were not so good, which told me that I had a lot to learn because these types of investment vehicles have many moving parts. However, if you understand how they work, they can be very powerful tools within a portfolio.

My wife, who was working for another company at the time, helped me build a presentation that allowed me to showcase my knowledge of these products to attendees. I paid all the marketing and other costs to attract prospects, and weeks later, I put on my first workshop geared toward annuities. I thought the industry had made these vehicles very difficult to understand, so I broke each annuity down on an individual basis, telling my audience the good, bad, and ugly of each one. An annuity is a vehicle that guarantees lifetime income. It's a promise between you and the insurance company offering that product. You provide the company with either a lump-sum payment or a flexible payment, and you are promised a return with conservative growth without the downside risk of the market. That first event went very well, and we received good feedback from individuals and couples taking advantage of our complimentary consultation. Over the next few weeks, we met with many of those prospects, and several became clients of the firm. I was paid directly by the insurance companies whose annuities I sold to clients. Then things got a little complicated with the firm. I had no marketing support from the firm and decided to fend for myself and not worry about their support to generate revenue for my family. I was excited to tell the firm's owner about the event and how successful it was, but the conversation didn't go as I expected. He felt entitled to 40% of the commission that I earned, but to me, our signed agreement said assets under management – investment assets that I brought into the firm. It said nothing about insurance-commissionable products. I argued that the document I signed in no way included insurance products. Our conversation got rather uncomfortable, to tell you the truth. I left the meeting and talked to some trusted colleagues that I could confide in, who had been around the block a time or two. After listening to me and looking at my agreement with the firm, they agreed that I was 100% correct.

I generated significant money for the firm at a 60/40 split even without the commissions, and without getting any support from the firm for my event, they wanted 40% of the revenue. I thought that was very unfair, especially after a year with the firm and doing as much as I did to bring in business. I saw it as a slap in the face. If we had agreed upon the 60/40 split on the investments under management and the insurance products in the agreement, that would be one thing. But annuities and life insurance were never discussed, and they aren't investments. These products are vehicles designed for safety, with guarantees, much like a CD or Money Market account. Sitting down with the owner was a little nerve-racking. He was a powerful man in the industry, and I didn't want to have any bad blood in the air. I came in prepared with the original documentation that we both signed and presented my argument as professionally and well planned as possible, but the conversation escalated very quickly. He wanted his cut, and there was no discussion needed as far as he was concerned. Finally, after being verbally threatened, I got up, walked out, and went home to draft my resignation letter. Even being somewhat new to the industry, I would not tolerate someone being disrespectful to me. And just like my reputation in the fire department, I wouldn't allow anyone to discredit my reputation in the financial industry. I handed in my resignation the following day, and just like that, I no longer had a home – again – where I could hang my financial adviser hat.

This time was different, though. I experienced three firms during my journey as a junior adviser and learned the ins and outs of how each one of these firms worked. I liked some things about each firm and other things I didn't and decided to think long and hard about my next move. I've always wanted to work for a company with a talented staff who knows their job well, in an organization that cares about the employees and clients, and whose process anyone could learn and be successful in the business. I think my firefighter career set the bar for this ideal company. Talking to Kate that night was one of the most fun, exciting, and scary times that we'd had up until that point in our relationship. We knew we had a great foundation started in our marriage. Kate worked as Marketing Coordinator for a governance company. I was an established firefighter and had a steady income from my adviser clients, so we discussed whether or not this was the right time to start my own firm. Kate said she could help on the branding and marketing side, and I could work on the process, structure, client relations, and acquisitions. After putting a framework together of how the business would work, including a cost breakdown of the company, we decided to move forward.

Filling the paperwork for the company and registering the firm was one of our biggest hurdles. The first thing that we had to do was choose a name for the LLC, but that wasn't too difficult. I'm a First Responder; being the first line of defense when people's homes are in danger is what I do every day. I wanted my firm to reflect that it would be the first line of defense in preserving and protecting our clients' money. The name FirstLine Financial came to me with ease!

CHAPTER 10

THE FIRM

KATE AND I WERE OFF AND RUNNING. We opened a business account and began looking for office space. I was doing a lot of the heavy lifting for the firm because Kate still had her full-time job as a Marketing Coordinator and had a nice income. She was there every step of the way, despite her full-time job, always supportive and encouraging, and I'd bounce ideas off her. Kate gave me recommendations that were always helpful, whether I implemented them or not. I was able to find an office not too far away from our home, and it was a nice space with all the amenities that we needed. Because not too many office spaces become available in this area, I jumped on it and signed a rental agreement. With the LLC established and approved and business banking accounts set up, I started to transition all my clients to FirstLine Financial. Transitioning was easy because I've built rapport and a trusting relationship with them. My reputation survived intact even after all of the ups and downs in my journey as a junior adviser.

I brought almost 100 accounts with me and started FirstLine Financial, managing approximately 10 million dollars worth of client's assets. I began defining the onboarding process and developed meetings with clients, learning from each firm in my journey. I feel these onboarding meetings are the most critical step in the business process to ensure that we fulfill our fiduciary responsibility to the clients. While working on this book, we trademarked our process as the W.R.A.P. Process, which stands for **W**ritten **R**etirement **A**ction **P**lan. We look at a client's current financial situation during the W.R.A.P. process, understand their goals and objectives, analyze their risk tolerance, and develop a customized financial plan to clarify the client's financial picture. We methodically laid out a four-step process.

The first step of the process is called our *Discovery Visit*. It is where the individual or family gets to know us by spending time in our office or on a phone call. We get to know about their lifestyle, family, health, work history, current savings, and future plans. It's important to get to know prospective clients to make sure our company is a good fit for them, and they are a good fit for FirstLine Financial. I've learned from many years of being an adviser that not everyone is the right fit for our firm. Though I'm an easy guy to get along with, I've seen a lot in my 40-plus years and need to learn as much as possible about the person sitting across the table from me before signing any contracts. I want to know what's important to them other than money because money is just a tool that allows us to do the things that are important to us. My job is not just to care about a return on investment – I care about getting a return on the client's retirement. I got into this business to change lives and allow my clients to live worry-free in their retirement years. I want to hear about their goals and objectives in life, where the prospective client came from, and what makes them tick. I watched clients sit down with advisers at the firms I'd worked for over the years and saw those advisers take over the meeting without allowing the client to speak up and share their situation.

My dad always said, *"Ryan, you have two ears and one mouth. You should be doing a lot more listening than talking,"* but I saw the opposite from these advisers. Those advisers would start talking about products and investments and what they could do for the client right out of the gate. Honestly, I felt like they were car salesmen who start pitching their vehicles as soon as anyone steps into the lot. I will never forget one of my first experiences with this when my aunt wanted help with her financial situation. She was retiring with a pension after many years with a great company. She had a healthy 401k and social security that she could rely on but asked me to sit down with her and go over her finances. I absolutely wanted to help, especially because she helped take care of my brother, sister, and me a lot when we were growing up. I asked my boss to sit in on the meeting with her, and his first question was about how much she had in her accounts and if her husband would be there. It seemed to me like he didn't care about my aunt and just cared about how much money she had. Not only that, he wanted to talk to her husband, assuming he was the decision-maker. He agreed to meet with us and when she came in, he joined us in the meeting room and I made the introduction. I barely got one sentence in, and he was off without even getting to know her. He didn't ask where she came from or how Ryan was as a boy growing up; there was no small talk, nothing. My aunt and I sat there while he went on a rant about everything he could provide to her. When he finished, the only thing he asked was if her husband would be joining us at the next meeting, which didn't matter because there was no second meeting. My aunt told me that she didn't want to be locked into a firm where the owner does all the talking and has no idea what's important to her. That meeting was an eye-opener for me. From that point forward in my career, I realized that it's all about the person sitting across the table from me. It's not about my agenda. What I do depends on connecting with the client, finding common ground, and respecting each other, which is why the Discovery Visit is so important. I want to make sure the client and I can form a relationship that will last a lifetime.

Case Study 1–
Lack of Safety and Protection

SITUATION

A 63-year-old male who worked for a chemical company his entire life was nearing retirement and needed to protect his 401k because that was the only money he had for a modest retirement.

CHALLENGE

After meeting with him and his wife, it was clear that they were loving and honest people because they brought her father into their home to care for him. In addition, their son still lived with them. Needless to say, it was a full house. With that on his mind, he was very adamant about protecting his retirement account. The only problem at this point was that his only retirement asset was sitting in the market without any protection.

OUTCOME

Because he was over 59 ½ years old, he had the opportunity to withdraw penalty-free from his 401k into an IRA account, allowing him to invest in other strategies that his 401k plan would otherwise not allow. Doing this opened the doors for him to entertain different strategies that would meet his desire to protect his retirement from the volatile market.

As I dove deep into his expenses, income, desired retirement age, liquid assets, risk tolerance, and his overall future goals, it was clear to me that we needed to take him out of the markets. Unfortunately, time was not on his side as he was within four years of retirement and a nervous nelly when it came to the stock market. I knew exactly what I needed to do, but it would take several visits for me to educate him on the strategy.

I met with him four times, and toward the last meeting, he felt very confident about my recommendation. Our next step was to get the paperwork going for the strategy, which protected the principle in his 401k assets—potential growth without being invested into the market and guaranteed income for life.

We constantly communicate with him and his family, who love receiving our printed quarterly newsletter and always appreciate reading updates on the company and our family. They said that receiving those updates makes them feel part of our growing family.

My mission statement is *to be the last adviser my clients ever work with.* After the Discovery Visit, I showcase the services that we offer and discuss if the client would like to move forward with us, but only if I feel they'd be a good fit for my firm. If both parties agree, we move forward to our second visit, called the Strategy Visit. After the prospect understands our process and what information we need to move forward, we'll set up a second meeting. When we've received all the necessary forms from the client and that second meeting is scheduled, we roll up our sleeves and get to work. This is when the actual value of FirstLine Financial begins to show. We spend between eight to twelve hours reviewing client documents then building and preparing a financial plan for them using some of the most sophisticated technology available today. Our goal is to make the financial strategies we build as easy to understand as possible yet diverse enough to provide the client with an appropriate amount of risk/reward suitable for their short and long-term needs to meet all of their goals and objectives. I don't just rely on my experiences with the three firms I worked for or what I learned to pass the Series 66 and Series 7 exams. Most firms ask things like *how much do you need when you retire to maintain your lifestyle?* If the prospective client says *I need five thousand dollars a month,* that becomes the basis for the client's plan recommendations. That is like responding to a fire and asking the homeowner what *you want us to do to save your home?* I tackle situations in life, including our approach to financial planning, using what I've learned in my 20 years as a firefighter. We assess each situation carefully so that we use the right tools for the circumstances and save lives, including our own.

At every fire scene, we implement an Incident Action Plan based on the specifics of the situation, which considers the amount and type of risk we're facing. I feel just as responsible about my obligation to the long-term financial health of our clients while doing these economic assessments and financial plans, so we dive much deeper into the client's lifestyle, family and employment history, current savings, as well as their "bucket list" goals and dreams. Once we have a better picture of the client's whole situation, we make sure that we use the right financial tools in the right way for the client's economic wellbeing. My job as an adviser has less to do with making money for my firm and everything to do with our clients' long-term wealth. Sometimes a successful and highly educated new client, say an engineer, comes to our first meeting with ideas of what he wants to invest in based on research, an article they read, or what friends have told them. Our firm won't just fill out paperwork for whatever the client had in mind.

I'm going a little deeper into a fundamental concept I discussed earlier that is confusing even to financial industry insiders. It's really important that readers of this book understand the word *fiduciary*. I'll start the confusing conversation by telling you that there is a "fiduciary responsibility." Individuals who hold this responsibility are called fiduciaries. This topic is so complicated that U.S. News and World Report published an article called *What Is a Fiduciary Financial Adviser?* [1] *A fiduciary is defined by the legal and ethical requirement to put your best interest before their own.* This article helps break down the Department of Labor's Fiduciary Rule recently approved by President Joe Biden's administration that went into effect on Feb. 16, 2021. I've included excerpts in the box below from this article to help you understand this chapter and recommend reading the article if you've got any investments or are thinking about working with a financial adviser now or in the future.

WHAT IS A FIDUCIARY?

A fiduciary is a person or legal entity, such as a bank or financial firm, that has the power and responsibility of acting for another (usually called the beneficiary or principal) in situations requiring total trust, good faith and honesty.

The most common example of a fiduciary is a trustee of a trust, but anyone can be a fiduciary. If you undertake to

---

1   US News and World Report *What Is a Fiduciary Financial Advisor?* By Coryanne Hicks April 15, 2021

assist someone in a situation where they place total confidence and trust in you, you have a fiduciary duty to that person. Corporate officers are fiduciaries for their shareholders, as are attorneys and real estate agents for their clients. Some, but not all, financial advisors are fiduciaries.

...."Pretend fiduciaries talk like fiduciaries to sound trusting, then they act like salesmen," says Knut Rostad, founder and president of the Institute for the Fiduciary Standard, a nonprofit that advocates for the fiduciary standard in McLean, Virginia....

As a fiduciary, I don't work for one company and sell only their financial products like bonds, stocks, or mutual funds. I research the best investment opportunity for that client and do what is necessary to add it to their portfolio. At FirstLine Financial, we educate our clients on the different *worlds of investing* and how each world has different characteristics. It is important to understand the characteristics of money to build a sound and purposeful portfolio strategy. So let's start there before we dive into the worlds of investing. The three characteristics of money that I talk about are safety, liquidity, and growth. The problem with investing is that you will only find one or two of the three characteristics in any investment. You will never find all three. You're always going to give up something, whether that is safety, liquidity, or growth in an investment. For example, If you want safety, you may open up a CD or Money Market account. In that investment vehicle, you are provided protection and liquidity. But what are you lacking? Growth. Every investment will have a pro, con, and strings attached. So we need to use multiple investments to access the three characteristics of money.

Now each characteristic of money falls within a category in what

I call the World of Investing. There are the Banking world, the Wall Street world, and the Alternative world. In the Banking world or the world of protection, you will find safety and liquidity two of the three characteristics. Your checking and savings accounts are liquid, which means they can easily be withdrawn as cash. The Banking world offers safety in the form of the Federal Deposit Insurance Corporation (FDIC) that provides protection of up to $250,000. Growth potential is not a characteristic of this world. Opposite of the Banking world is the Wall Street world or the world of potential where you will find liquidity and growth but not a lot of safety. This world includes the stock market, and people often don't realize that it's liquid, meaning the investment can be sold and withdrawn as cash quickly. This world can show significant growth at around ten to fifteen percent or even more, but it depends one-hundred percent on the stocks in the portfolio. The Alternative world or the predictable world can be viewed as a hybrid blend between the Banking world and the Wall Street world. It gives you some of the safety and security like in the Banking world but also provides better growth potential like the Wall Street world. What it lacks is liquidity because there is usually a time commitment with these vehicles. These investment vehicles are relatively safe and offer conservative returns in the range of six to eight percent, which is more growth than the Banking world but not as much as the Wall Street world.

We often spend an entire appointment discussing the various products that we're suggesting to the client. We want them to understand the risk factor and potential reward of each. I consider our relationship much like a business. The client is the Chief Executive Officer of his investment portfolio, and I am the Chief Financial Officer (CFO). It's my responsibility as CFO to make sure the CEO knows everything he or she needs to know to make decisions on where to put their money. First, I make sure they understand their current financial picture and explain how it might look in the future when it's their primary source of funds. Then we dive into the various options we propose to preserve and grow their retirement portfolio.

We strive to teach our clients about market volatility and the correlation between their portfolio and the market. One of the things I had to experience on my own in 2008 is the trade-off between risk vs. reward. I learned that because of my investment in the luxury waterfront condo that I invested in with my brother. Not only did I lose my home during the financial crash, but I also lost almost forty percent of my retirement savings. As tough as that time in my life was, it taught me that the markets are uncertain. I realized then that I was in deep trouble if I needed that money to last throughout my retirement years, and that lesson has been passed on to our clients. Let's say a client is supplementing income by taking four or five percent out of their portfolio when markets are trending downward. The reality is that the portfolio's base is shrinking. There will be less money, when markets rebound, than expected because the four or five percent return was calculated against a shrinking portfolio. Some advisers have coined this phenomenon as *Reverse Dollar Cost Averaging*. It's the opposite of Dollar Cost Averaging, which is buying into the market at different intervals in the accumulation phase of your life.

In 2020, as I write this book, we are experiencing one of the most unprecedented times the market has ever seen. For almost eleven years, the market had been going up after the Dow Jones Industrial Average fell 777.68 points in one day during the financial crash of 2008. "Prior to the 2020 crash, the Dow had just reached its record high of 29,551.42 on February 12. From that peak to the March 9 low, the Dow Jones Industrial Average (DJIA) lost 5,700.40 points or 19.3%. It had narrowly avoided the 20% decline that would have signaled the start of a bear market."[2] The coronavirus completely shut

---

2   How Does the 2020 Stock Market Crash Compare With Others? BYKIMBERLY AMADEO May 09, 2021 www.TheBalance.

the economy down, many small businesses closed, and hundreds of thousands filed for unemployment. It was a very uncertain time in our country, and in 2021 things are slowly getting better, but people are still scared. *Sequence of return risk* is a fancy phrase that means retiring during times of economic instability like 2000, 2001, 2008, and 2020 into a steeply declining market, which I experienced in 2008. Not only will the declining market reduce the value of your portfolio, but there's also a chance you'll need to sell your investments at their lowest value. This is why talking through your portfolio and how market volatility hurts it, sometimes more than it helps, is an important topic that we have to discuss. We show clients how much risk they're taking for each asset or asset class. We can measure the risk of their portfolio and compare that to the current market. Not only that, we show clients how much they could lose should we experience extreme market corrections. We use a very powerful tool to do that kind of analysis. Most people we meet with have never seen their portfolio dissected like this. It's like a doctor's office where the doctor's staff takes the patient's blood pressure and vitals before the patient meets with the doctor to give the doctor information on their general health. We do the same with client portfolios and have data in hand about the health of their assets to discuss with them.

After discussing critical or significant concepts in these meetings, I bring everything together in an easy-to-understand diagram. We want our clients to understand the current status of their portfolios and show them what strategies we have in mind to grow and protect their assets. We look at a portfolio like it's a house: it must have a good foundation, insulation in the walls, and a roof to protect what's inside for many years to come. Each part of the construction of a newly designed home will require different tools as well as different materials. The same holds true in portfolio management. You wouldn't

com

want to use wood shingles in fire-prone areas; you'll have a high-risk factor and may not be able to insure the house. Like designing a home, we break down each asset and discuss what it's intended to do in the overall construction of the portfolio. I often hear people say I like this investment or that investment in meetings who don't yet understand that it is just one piece in the overall puzzle of a plan. Going back to the house metaphor, if the builder says *no problem* to the wood shingle roof, that house may not survive next summer's fire season. We don't say yes to every investment people say they like without ensuring it serves a purpose in their overall portfolio. While constructing a client's portfolio, something we have to discuss with people who have worked for twenty, thirty, or forty years is the fact that they have several retirement accounts in different places. A 401k here, an IRA there, or a savings account or two in places they've forgotten about. We ask a series of questions that bring clarity to the person's financial picture and help them know where all their money is and what it's doing for them. They start to see their fiscal home coming together. We often see a client's eyes light up because seeing their whole financial picture laid out like this is something that most people haven't seen. The final aha moment for those who visit with us is when we put everything together and show them whether they will be successful by keeping their current strategy versus working with us. Sometimes people feel bad that they want to "divorce" their adviser of several years, and I offer a few ways to do that after we've completed the visit. Our firm's success rate usually convinces those on the fence; typically, we can assure them a high probability of success if they follow our philosophy.

CASE STUDY 2 – ANNUITY TRAP SITUATION

A couple in their early 60s; the husband is retired from the U.S. Postal Service, and the wife is a veterinarian who owns an animal clinic. This couple was heavily weighted in annuity products.

CHALLENGE

After getting to know the Veterinarian and her husband, we dove into their portfolio and determined that 92% of their investments were products that provide safety but offer limited growth. In addition, between the two of them, they had a total of nine annuity policies.

The couple expressed the desire to be more aggressive with their portfolio, which was my sentiment exactly. So we took advantage of the 10% penalty-free withdrawal on all of their annuities and invested the monies into a more growth-oriented strategy.

OUTCOME

Their portfolio is no longer over-weighted in annuity policies, is now truly diversified, and has potential for more growth. The Veterinarian and her husband are very pleased with their portfolio and appreciate having gone through the W.R.A.P. Process with us. Their first annual review is in a few months, and we are looking forward to showing them the progress so far.

The Strategy Visit is usually long and runs between an hour and forty-five minutes to two and one-half hours. I don't rush this visit because it's where the rubber meets the road. If we have a meaningful conversation addressing their goals and objectives, we allow time for them to make an educated decision about what they want to fix or ignore. If they feel comfortable moving into the 3rd visit, that's where we start Automated Customer Account Transfer Service (ACATS), the transfer of their accounts to our firm. After completing this step, we schedule the implementation visit and look at the client's plan. We start by looking at the big picture as if looking at a landscape from the airplane window, then dig into each recommended strategy specifically for the client's situation, going deeper into each investment one at a time. Every client is different, and we take a very customized approach when building our client portfolios. We don't just pick out five or six of our favorite funds to get a client's money into the market and call it a day like some larger brokerage shops do for a quick commission. We use many different types of investment vehicles and like to showcase our knowledge. Unlike familiar brokerage firms that most people recognize from their advertisements, we don't sell a fixed number of investment products. We are constantly learning about new offerings that we research to ensure they have a track record of performing well. We vet the investment, and the company offering that investment vets us, which is a time-consuming process. But that is how I find the best offerings available for our client's specific needs. We like to use alternative investments, a tool that I will discuss in more detail in the following chapter. But throughout the implementation visit, we check in with the client to make sure they understand what we're explaining. During the session I often say, *Are you with me? Do you understand? Do you have any questions?* because we're talking about their life savings. I want to make sure that the client has complete certainty about the process and understands the structure we are designing for them. Sometimes it requires two meetings to get through the implementation of their plan. We can spend two hours discussing ideas or the what-ifs of their plan. If they're not comfortable with what's being presented, we schedule another visit because we don't want to rush this part of the process. Taking our time allows the client to sort everything out, which means we have a better chance of keeping that client for life.

I remember how little I knew about the industry when I started.

Even after being in the industry for a few years, my colleagues would talk about a product or a tool they used for their clients, and I would pretend that I knew what they were talking about. The truth is, sometimes I had no idea and lost them after the first five minutes of the conversation, and that's not what I want for my clients. I know some people move slower than others because I was a very slow learner in school – so slow in elementary school that I was pulled out of my class and didn't understand why I was taken to a different room with a few other students. I thought to myself, *Why am I in here? Am I special?* Yes, I was special and sent to special education for students who learned slower than the other students. I developed slowly, and my life didn't come together until well into my 20s when I started to apply myself. Then things finally paid off. So I have compassion for clients who struggle with all of this complicated financial planning information. When the client has confidence in the strategy, we begin to reallocate their portfolio from where they've been to where we're placing them. We don't sell anything until our client gives us the discretion to move forward; remember, we look at ourselves as the CFO of our client's wealth. They are the CEO of their money and are always in control. We are there to navigate the ship while they're on board and want them to enjoy the journey.

After the plan is implemented, it's all about staying connected with the client and providing as much value through quarterly or annual reviews. We stay connected through client appreciation events or holiday parties – we like to do things a little differently than other firms out there. One of the things we enjoy is the annual retreat with our top ten clients. We rent a few cabins right next to one of the ski resorts in Utah and offer them to our clients on a first-come, first-served basis and are booked in a matter of hours. We'll host a dinner at one of the resorts with an open bar and mingle the rest of the night to enjoy catching up with each other. It's one of our most memorable events that clients talk about for weeks after.

The final phase of our W.R.A.P. Process is the Completion Visit, where we sit down and deliver our W.R.A.P. Organizer to new clients. The Organizer contains everything we have presented and worked out for the client, separated into tabs so the client can go straight to the section they want. It gives them the roadmap to their financial future. If the client has questions, we go directly to the Organizer, and I'll review documents that we created to help the client see how the game plan is moving forward. We look at all aspects of the client's life throughout our process. We will talk about having an income plan so that clients understand the money coming through their door. We look at investment planning and investment management to know how the portfolio is positioned and, most importantly, why. Taxes are a big topic of conversation in our office, so we talk through tax strategies and ways to legally and ethically *disinherit* the government from the client's wealth. Wealth transfer, where the client wants their money to go, is another subject that we spend time on, which other firms commonly overlook. We focus and devote time to many other things that give our clients confidence that their retirement goals and objectives will be met throughout their retirement years.

CHAPTER 11

A DIFFERENT APPROACH TO INVESTING

A FEW YEARS INTO RUNNING MY FIRM, I met a gentleman named Bill Gross, not the co-founder of PIMCO. This Bill is Managing Director for a division of Raymond James called Alex Brown. Mr. Gross had managed the New York franchise baseball league's money for some time. He was a presenter at a conference that I was invited to. Listening to his presentation, Mr. Gross seemed to know more than the average adviser. The speaker mentioned several different kinds of investments, called *alternatives,* that he used to manage portfolios for a wealthy family who owned a baseball team. As Mr. Gross went through his presentation, he kept discussing alternatives. I had never been exposed to concepts like private equity which allows various investors to invest in small, young firms that could be advanced and improved that can later be sold at a high price. This is done to obtain large-scale profit. Think of Shark Tank, where these young firms look for Mr. Wonderful to buy into their company for an obvious piece of the action by giving them an influx of capital to scale their business plan. Private debt is a little different. It's a loan that can be informal or formal. The debt does not allow huge investment in the company. It is provided by an individual or company, depending upon the relation of the debtor and the creditor. Venture capital (VC) is a form of private equity, a type of financing that investors provide to startup[3] companies and small businesses believed to have long-term growth[4] potential. Venture capital[5] generally comes from wealthy investors, investment banks, other financial institutions, or a Business Development Company (BDC). This organization invests in small and medium-sized companies as well as distressed companies. With distressed businesses, the BDC helps the companies regain sound financial footing. Then we have absolute return investing, opportunity zones, and natural resources. I will explain more in-depth in a second book geared specifically at looking at all alternative investments. But

---

3   https://www.investopedia.com/terms/s/startup.asp

4   https://www.investopedia.com/terms/l/longtermgrowth.asp

5   https://www.investopedia.com/ask/answers/062315/what-type-funding-options-are-available-private-company.asp

using these investment strategies and vehicles has been developed and successfully employed by many of the world's wealthiest and most successful university endowments, institutions and private wealth managers across the globe. Endowments and institutions, with very large amounts of money at stake and very substantial intellectual capital, believed there was a better way to excel in a rapidly changing world. They developed an approach often referred to as the "endowment strategy," which deviates from the traditional stock and bond models of yesteryear.

I was perplexed thinking: *Why haven't I been exposed to these types of investments before?* After his presentation, I didn't have an opportunity to connect with him. In fact, no one did because he was hopping on a plane flying back to his home in New York. For the rest of the conference, I was baffled by his speech. I had spent over a year and a half studying and thought I had learned everything I needed to know about investing, but I was wrong! After returning home from the conference, my mission became to track down the presenter's number so I could have a conversation with him. It wasn't easy, but I got through to him and asked if I could have fifteen to twenty minutes of his time. I was prepared if he said yes, with five to ten questions on hand to ask him. I started firing the questions at him, and he was very articulate in his answers. *Ryan, I was where you are 30 years ago;* he said and told me that most advisers are playing the same game: they are on a hamster wheel, always looking for the next client. He said *you need to redefine your value proposition and present what many advisers don't understand.* I asked about all these other tools that he talked about, the alternatives he discussed. He told me to look around and see what the largest families, pension funds, endowments, and sovereign wealth funds do with their money. He assured me that they have a small percentage in the stock market, but what these organizations strive to do is increase return while decreasing volatility – what all advisers try to do when building portfolios. And what I've learned about volatility and the stock market is that people feel the pain of losses; more than they enjoy the pleasures of gains. He explained that these fund managers work particularly hard to build portfolios containing various alternative investments that allow them to build out truly non-correlated portfolios.

That means that they try to craft a portfolio using different asset classes or sectors using both traded and non-traded/off-market investments. The goal is that when one asset class or sector doesn't do well, another asset class or sector in that portfolio is performing well in the market. Think of it like a golf tournament where there's a leaderboard of professional golfers. Similarly, there's a leader board of global asset classes. In any given day, week, year, or ten-to-twenty-year period, there are global asset classes, advanced markets, and sophisticated economies fighting to be in the top position of this leader board. Sometimes they will be at the top, sometimes they're in the middle, and sometimes they're at the bottom. The reason we use these different asset classes is to stay diversified because, just like golfers who want to be at the top, we don't want client portfolios falling to the bottom. It's a tough place to be. Advisers and brokers like portfolios to fall somewhere in the middle, so they will introduce bonds into the mix of assets so that if equities go down, bonds will most likely go up. So they say. I will touch on this philosophy later. But first, I saw an illustration that shows correlation well, and we've recreated it here.

A once diverse portfolio using a 60/40 model, where stocks represented 60% of the portfolio and bonds represented 40%, viewed as a non-correlated asset having a positive and negative correlation, was once attractive to investors. That is not the case anymore from what we saw in 2008 when investment corporate grade bonds lost 5.3%. In fact, in an article written in Investment News, Dan Jamieson showcased a warning by FINRA cautioning investors on the risk associated with holding bonds or bond funds because of the rising interest rate environment that we are currently in. Ray Dalio, one of the most prolific investors over the last decade or two and the founder of Bridgewater Associates, the world's largest hedge-fund firm, echoed the same warning and is not a fan of bonds. In a quote, he said, *The economics of investing in bonds (and most financial assets) has become stupid... Rather than get paid less than inflation why not instead buy stuff — any stuff — that will equal inflation or better?[6]* — Ray Dalio

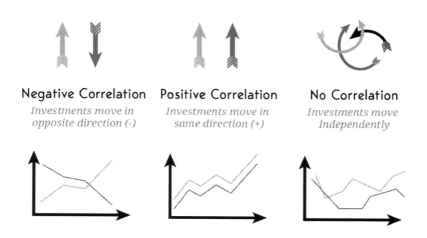

Negative Correlation
Investments move in opposite direction (-)

Positive Correlation
Investments move in same direction (+)

No Correlation
Investments move Independently

In 2020 bonds did not perform like they used to, much like in 2008. Bill Gross also told me that you need to look at non-correlated positions to have a winning strategy. So, if you can't get assets with zero correlation in the markets, you need to go somewhere else. That is why large institutions and endowments seek out alternatives or off-market investments. This type of investment can get a potentially

6   https://www.marketwatch.com/story/investing-in-bonds-has-become-stupid-ray-dalio-says-heres-what-he-recommends-in-stead-11615863155

better return with considerably less risk. He told me that alternative investments were only for high rollers for many years because they have enough money to be accredited, which means they either make two to three-hundred-thousand dollars annually for a certain number of years or have a net income of one-million-dollars.

That means they have a lot of money; however, times are changing. What was once meant for the very few is now being offered to the masses. You don't need to be a high net-worth accredited investor to get access. The rules have changed, and anyone can buy into an alternative investment even if they are not accredited. I won't go into much detail about alternative investments in this chapter because it's a vast topic with special considerations, which is why I plan to write a book specifically about this subject in the future. It's an exciting time in the world of investing, and I'm glad that I attended that conference with Bill Gross and even happier that I could connect with him afterward. In that phone call, we also talked through some of the allocations the big institutions had in their portfolio, which are overweighed in alternative companies to equities. If you follow the U.S. stock market, it declined nearly 40% in 2008, and the broad stock market was negative over a ten-year period. A broad market index is most characterized by including stocks from companies of all sizes. Stocks are divided into the classes of large, mid, and small-cap based on the values of the companies according to their stock prices and total outstanding shares. The widely followed stock indexes, the DJIA and S&P 500, are composed of only large-cap stocks. A broad market index includes stocks from all three size categories.

Still, many endowments and institutions enjoyed success during these same periods. At the end of our call, I knew I had a lot still to learn. I began digging into some of the alternative vehicles he mentioned and reached out to different companies to inquire about what they offered. I performed a crazy amount of due diligence on each of the offerings that I was interested in before presenting them to clients. I was overwhelmed and knew that this was a space that I needed to spend a lot of time learning about. I picked up a few books on investing in alternatives that had been recently published and read them all cover to cover. A book called "Wise Money" was everything I was looking for to understand the ins and outs of this space. That book broke down each alternative vehicle in detail. The author, Daniel Wildermuth, also talked about the outdated 60/40 model and how broken it was, but after 2008, nothing changed in the retail space of investing. Brokers continued to push this outdated model even after what they saw in that record-breaking financial crash. Most investors had to delay retirement and put their dreams on hold.

As I write this sitting here today during the COVID-19 pandemic of 2020-21, I'm looking at the vast majority of investors who have lost thirty percent of their wealth so far. Unfortunately, I'm not sure if we've seen the bottom yet. It took the S&P 500 twenty-two trending days to fall thirty percent from its record high reached on Feb. 19th of 2020[7], making it the fastest drop of this magnitude in history. The closest thing to this downfall happened during the Great Depression. In July 1932, the Dow Jones Industrial Average was down eighty-nine percent. Having seen a thirty percent drop so far this year, knowing there's no cure for COVID-19 and it's not even remotely controlled, it's safe to say, or at least to acknowledge, that the market could still drop considerably more.

This concerns me because some of my clients don't have twenty-five years to recover, which it took to recoup losses after the Great Depression. For this reason, I dedicated myself to learning everything I could about alternatives. I'm not here to say that I know everything about alternatives, but I do have the right people I can turn to who have answers, and I have an "always learning" mindset. For example, I

---

7   https://www.cnbc.com/2020/02/19/stock-market-wall-street-in-focus-amid-coronavirus-outbreak.html

learned of a broker/dealer who specializes in alternative investments — a broker/dealer is a company that offers products from outside sources to investment advisers associated with their platform. Surprisingly enough, the broker/dealer was the author of the book I had just finished reading, so I reached out to Mr. Wildermuth and spent a lot of time learning about his business model. After a few trips to meet the firm's owners and their team, I signed an agreement with them to solicit business through their firm. I have to say it was one of the best moves I made during that very early stage of my career. Not only did I become a better adviser, but I also had people around me who believed in the business model that I became so passionate about. My firm was doing very well and growing at a steady pace. In fact, my wife, Kate, resigned from her full-time job in marketing, started working for the company, and is an important and much-needed part of the business. She took on many projects, helped systematize paperwork, accounting, and created a brand logo that I'm so proud of. We plan to do many events over the next few years to get our message out to prospective investors and soon-to-be retirees. I think everyone needs to hear the presentation.

There was a time when I thought there were only a few tools I could use to build or craft a retirement portfolio. As I learn about this business, my firm continues to evolve with different product offerings and investment vehicles. I hear, now and then, that certain products are good or bad and learn that advisers sometimes discredit one vehicle over another. There is no silver bullet, no magic product, or portfolio that will get everyone through their retirement years. Every product out there, like people, has a good side, a bad side, and a string attached, which is why we don't discriminate on products. We love all investment vehicles and work hard to find just the right one for each situation. If I were going to build a house and picked only one tool to do the job, that house would very likely have some rough edges. I can't use a hammer to cut a piece of wood or a screwdriver to weld a pipe, and I can't use a saw to nail in baseboards. Different projects call for different tools, just like a retirement plan needs different products to do certain things. This is why we are a full-service financial firm that doesn't restrain our clients from doing what they want. We are all about working together with the client and finding the right strategy for their situation. Alternative investments have, over time, attempted to provide a portfolio with more non-correlated asset classes than just traded securities. Most alternative investments are non-traded, meaning you will not find them on the market. This allows them to have lower correlation or, in some cases, zero correlation to the markets. This strategy is not known by most investors. It is used only by a few knowledgeable advisers because the key to a successful retirement is to include more asset classes than what is typically used in an individual investor's portfolio. The goal throughout our process is to educate our clients about options available to them. Most financial advisers are simply not educated in alternatives. Sometimes, it's those things in life that we don't know that cause some doubt or fear. I believe that fear is good; it's a survival instinct and will always be there. Life taught me that we need to embrace it.

CASE STUDY 3 –
TRUE DIVERSIFICATION

SITUATION

59-year-old male who worked as an engineer at Boeing and wanted to retire soon but didn't have a plan.

CHALLENGE

After sitting down with the gentleman and his wife during their first visit with me, it was clear that they were doing fine. I gauge a prospective client on how they've done with their retirement accounts. Well, this man and his wife had won the game. They did everything by the book and to top it off, he had a pension which is becoming rarer every day. My challenge was that he was heavily weighted in the stock market and only one year away from retirement. I completed a portfolio analysis using our financial planning software and exposed a potential loss of 31% or $329,000 if a financial crisis happened again. In addition, there was no true diversity within his portfolio.

OUTCOME

They were the ideal W.R.A.P. client. We diversified their portfolio, which included assets within each structure of the fiscal home; roof, walls, and foundation. The philosophy behind the fiscal home is to allow each element of the house to work independently with its own goals and objectives.

We utilized the penalty-free withdrawal in his 401k and put his money into a Rollover IRA to allow for better strategies to meet his moderate approach to growth in the roof. A portion of his portfolio was placed into the walls where he would invest in different non-traded securities called alternative investments. Principle protection was established as the foundation to protect his wealth and hard-earned money.

Along with the W.R.A.P. analysis of his savings, we also analyzed their social security and determined the best time to start taking it.

They were very happy to have a retirement plan in place. We meet with them on an annual basis to catch up and also to review their portfolio. The client is enjoying retirement and has been hard at work crossing off items on his honey-do list. His wife is still happily working. They live a comfortable life where they can travel and see their children and grandchildren.

CHAPTER 12

THE FAMILY OFFICE

OVER THE YEARS, I HAVE seen many different business models in the financial industry. Believe me when I say that not all of them are created equal, nor are all investment brokers or financial planners a true "fiduciary." There are as many licenses to sell financial products as there are investments to buy. Some investment firms represent investment groups, some are licensed insurance agents, and some are like me. I am an investment adviser representative working for my own independent Registered Investment Adviser or RIA in the state of Arizona. I invested in programs and people to help me learn what I needed to know so I could take and pass many license exams. All of that gives me the knowledge and expertise to introduce my clients to investment market opportunities that best serve them instead of presenting to the client the investment product that best helps me.

I want to take time and review the different licenses that people in the financial industry can get in-depth. An insurance license is entirely different from having a securities license. The insurance test consists of a hundred questions and can be quickly completed in a few days. People who get an insurance license most likely work as captive agents and are educated on a handful of proprietary products through the insurance company they represent before hitting the streets looking for business. Insurance agents sit down with people who have worked their entire lives to accumulate wealth and present one or two products to solve the prospective client's problems. I see a problem with that, and just to reiterate what I also believe – these are not bad people or bad companies. I represent insurance companies but am not an employee or captive agent who's limited to selling only their products. I'm an independent working through my firm. I am not biased toward one insurance company or one product. I can work with any insurance company out there. If their product is suitable for my client, we will look at it. But I never pitch just one company or one product to make a sale. I look at the whole financial picture before selecting any product. First, we establish the client's wants, needs, and goals then start building a comprehensive plan based on those personal objectives. Some insurance products carry fees and are usually not liquid products. I'm not lumping all products together in this discussion. I'm talking about a few vehicles, specifically insurance products. Personally, I love life insurance and annuities, but the investment has to be effective for the client. They need to understand what they're getting into. I have seen so many instances where clients sit down with me and have no idea what they bought or the terms they were signed up for. It's unfortunate because, if explained correctly, clients would feel highly confident about the purchase. Once again, I want to make sure you understand that *these insurance products are very powerful tools* but have received negative press. Often, agents do not explain them correctly in a rush to make the sale.

Next are the brokers of the world who are generally licensed securities advisers and work for a large wirehouse[8] or brokerage firm. These advisers have been through the same testing process that I went through. I have a lot of respect for these individuals because the tests are extremely difficult, which means they've spent time educating themselves on the industry. They have passed the Series 7, Series 66, and maybe the Series 65 test, which is another exam and license required for individuals to act as an investment adviser. The main difference is that they work for an institution that hasn't adopted a fiduciary standard and therefore falls under the suitability standard. What does *suitability standard* mean exactly? You first must understand that advisers are held to different ethical standards for managing people's money. Advisers who work under the suitability standard only make recommendations suitable for clients regarding their financial needs, objections, and unique circumstances. The suitability standard is generally applied to broker-dealers, working under a broker and representing only

---

8   Wirehouse: a term used to describe a full-service broker-dealer. Modern-day wirehouses range from small regional brokerages to large institutions with global footprints. The term was coined when brokerage firms were connected to their branches primarily through private telephone and telegraph wires. Source: *Investopedia.com*

their products, who facilitate trades for their clients and receives a commission which is their sales model.

To summarize, investments offered under the suitability standard need to be suitable for the end investor, not necessarily what is best for the client. I have a little problem with this. Unless you live under a rock, you can remember the 2008 market crash. There is a movie called *The Big Short* that explains it perfectly. I highly recommend watching that movie if you haven't seen it. Getting back to the point, the film explains in laymen's terms that the 2008 crash was the result of bad investments in the form of mortgage-backed securities (MBS). In short, MBS are just a bunch of junk mortgages packaged together and sold to consumers like you and me. Brokers were selling these packaged products, slapping an A+ rating on them, and it was ok because they were *suitable*, even though the brokers knew that they were junk. So what was in these packaged products? Bad mortgages that banks allowed to slip through the cracks because of their low lending standards. In the end, when mortgage defaults began rolling in, investors were left holding a worthless piece of paper.

Another type of adviser is an independent fiduciary who is required to uphold a *fiduciary standard*. A fiduciary comes from the Latin term for trust. It simply means they have a legal, ethical, and moral obligation to put your best interest first. We, as fiduciaries, are required to put your interest ahead of any brokerage firm, sales managers, board of directors, and profits. Whereas, if you work for a broker, you need to put the company's best interest first because they participate in what's called revenue sharing, which means it's a pay-to-play game. Fiduciaries follow the investment advisory model. These advisers are fee-based and make their money through fees charged on assets under management (AUM). This fee is disclosed on the A.D.V. form, which the client will receive when they conduct business with an advisory firm. Fiduciary advisers are held to the highest standard and are required to put their client's interests above their own. Another difference within this fiduciary model is that an adviser or financial planner can do business on a fee-only basis. Some planners charge a fixed price and are not motivated by selling products. Their goal is to build the best plan possible for the client and will be compensated for that plan based on its value. After learning about the many types of financial planners and adviser business models in use, it was an easy choice for me when I was deciding to set up shop. The investment advisory model, known as the fiduciary model, was a lot cleaner. It felt better to me, and if you really think about what it does for the relationship between the adviser and the client, this business model puts everybody on the same side of the table. It aligns client and adviser's interests in the same direction – doing what's best for the client's long-term financial health. Using the fiduciary investment advisory model, what's best for you is best for me and vice versa.

If I'm a fee-based adviser making money through fees agreed to at the beginning of the relationship with a client, and if their portfolio drops in value, guess what? I take a pay cut as well. The only way for me to make more money is to increase the value of the client's account. If the client and I have agreed that my fee is one percent, then one percent of $200,000 is a lot more than one percent of $100,000, right? I want to make it very clear how people in the financial industry make money. Just because an adviser walks into someone's home or talks to them on the phone and says they are a fiduciary, my advice is what my dad always said, *you can't believe everything everyone tells you.* It's in the client's best interest to do some digging to find out more about the individual who wants to take care of their savings. Their name can often be searched on BrokerCheck.com, a service offered by FINRA, the non-governmental organization established by Congress to oversee the securities industry, the same people whose grueling tests I had to pass to get licensed. If an adviser holds the appropriate licenses to become a true fiduciary, that website will tell you. The record on

Broker Check will show either the Series 7 with the Series 66 license or a Series 65 license and should be working as an independent adviser. If they are working for a wirehouse or brokerage house, then they are not truly a fiduciary and are working under the suitability standard model we discussed earlier in this chapter. Working with a fiduciary offers more growth potential because these advisers are required to put the client's interest first. It took me quite a bit of time to understand what this meant –being a true fiduciary who lives up to the fiduciary standard and works as an independent adviser versus a broker who follows the suitability standard - and I was working in the business! The simple truth is that many people don't know the difference, so it's important to spread this message to the public.

Now that we've established the difference between agents, brokers, and fiduciaries, let's look at another title, the *Registered Representative*. A registered representative is a person who works for a brokerage company and serves as a representative for clients trading products such as stocks, bonds, mutual funds, and alternative products. They are registered through FINRA and governed by the suitability standard. I was a registered representative at one time, so I could be called a broker in a sense. But I was working for independent firms with an affiliation with a broker/dealer — confused yet? For a few years, I worked for independent companies that were still charging commissions because of their affiliation with a broker/dealer. After conversations with my peers and a lot of additional education, I created my own RIA, a Registered Investment Adviser. An RIA is an investment firm registered either with the State or Securities Exchange Commission (SEC) and must adhere to the investment advisers act of 1940. In the RIA model, we do not receive any type of commission. We are true fiduciaries and fee-based. Owning my own RIA, I work as an IAR or Investment Adviser Representative under the RIA. So, even though I'm the owner and founder of FirstLine Financial, I'm still an IAR under the firm. Still, I make all the decisions about what products or vehicles I bring in to service my clients. Since I'm the Chief Compliance Officer, I hold all the risks in an audit. This is why doing due diligence on what is offered through the firm is so important. I am ultimately responsible for implementing a client's retirement plan. Using the right vehicles is of the utmost importance to live up to my fiduciary responsibility, which is why I scour the financial market to see what others like me are using successfully in their client's portfolios.

I was told about a conference in Canada shortly after setting up my RIA. This conference was geared specifically toward RIAs and Family Offices. I learned that attendees need to have $100 million in assets under management to qualify for the event. I quickly told the acquaintance who told me of this event that I was nowhere near that amount. He said, "what are friends for" before putting in a call to the event host. About twenty minutes later, I received an email inviting me to Montreal. I could not believe it! I gladly accepted as I had no clue what to expect, so with very short notice, I scrambled to get an updated passport because mine had expired. I had to pay for an expedited passport to get it in time, and then I was off to Montreal. I stayed in a beautiful hotel overlooking a few small restaurants and saw lots of people enjoying themselves. After checking in at the registration desk, I received a packet and a schedule of events, then went up to my room and got ready for cocktail hour that evening. People were already mingling when I arrived, but I didn't know anyone, so I just got busy doing what I was there to do – figure things out! Having just formed my own RIA and being shoulder-to-shoulder with some of the largest RIA's in the world, I wanted to make the most of this moment. So I grabbed a drink, put a smile on my face, and started introducing myself to anyone who made eye contact with me. It was an inspiring night full of interesting conversation, fantastic entertainment, and tasty food. I gathered a stack of business cards that night from different firms and, after the cocktail hour, rushed upstairs to my room and made notes on each card. I wanted to make sure I remembered whom I talked to and what they did if I ran into them in the future.

Two things I heard that night frequently from those I talked to were *I have a single-family office*, or *I have a multi-family office*. Those were phrases that I had never heard before, had no idea what they meant, nodded my head, and went along with whatever was said. It was a little intimidating because I was very naive and in awe of the people surrounding me. I talked to some RIAs, asked what they specialized in and what brought them out to the conference. Most of the RIAs I spoke with were well-established firms with a very healthy book of business and well known in the industry. I asked a lot of the same questions to everyone I spoke with – I wanted to know how they structured their practice. Most attendees told me they were there to network and learn about the alternative products being showcased. I turned -in relatively early that first night because I knew I had a long couple of days ahead, full of powerful information sharing from experts in the industry. I wanted to be well-rested and at my best. The next day I geared up in a new suit, tie, and shoes. I went all out for this conference! Image is everything, and coming from the fire department, where I wore the same blue uniform for twenty years, I was excited to get dressed up for a change. It felt almost like I had another identity because sometimes I feel a little like Superman during my business day. I come from years living a fireman's life, where it's all about rushing to the fire truck, donning my personal protection equipment, jumping out of the truck to battle some type of fire, or responding to an EMS call, where I'm grabbing all of the EMS equipment and entering a scene where I have to keep a cool head at all times. That is a massive contrast to the financial industry, where it's about presenting yourself well and showing up like you belong. It took me a while to wrap my head around that identity change happening on so many days. But these days, whether I'm in my fire suit or my business suit, I'm as comfortable gearing up for a big meeting or speaking at a conference as I am jumping into an emergency or talking to strangers about fire safety at a community event.

The morning of the conference started with various presentations explaining several products that we can use in our financial planning toolbox. Many of the vehicles discussed I had never heard of, like interval funds, opportunity zones, private equity, and venture capital. It felt like drinking water out of a fire hose, and I had to be ready to swallow as much as I possibly could. I know how that feels! One of the most exciting presentations for me was by a CPA and an ex-hedge fund manager. They spoke about family offices and the impact they have on the industry. One introduced what a family office was and talked about some powerful, wealthy families who amassed fortunes from real estate, technology, oil & gas, and even beer. The people he mentioned were in the room with us and were people I had spoken to the previous night over cocktails. I had no idea the kinds of people that were in the room with me that evening! I began googling names and companies mentioned and could not believe that I was surrounded by so much wealth. I'm not talking a couple of million dollars. These were first, second, and third-generation families who've been able to preserve and grow their wealth year after year, decade after decade, generation after generation. I was overwhelmed and couldn't help but wonder what I was doing there and why I deserved to be there? Sometimes we do not give ourselves the credit we deserve and question who we are, what we stand for, and if we belong. I assure you that those thoughts were running through my mind for the rest of the conference. I realized that I might never be able to attend another one of these events based on my book of business alone. I was so blessed to be invited by the host, one of the nicest, most down-to-earth gentlemen I have ever met. I didn't hold back any punches throughout that conference. I was scared, of course, but I put myself out there and talked to these established, wealthy families. I asked question after question, wanting to know what these single and multi-family offices were doing with their wealth. I learned that a single-family office (SFO) is one family that's amassed a great deal of wealth and manages that wealth in a couple of different ways. The first way is by not losing money by taking calculated risks and doing tons of due diligence. They have a dedicated team of professional advisers who oversee clients' complete financial affairs. Just like a successful business brings together disciplines to work cooperatively, families with substantial wealth must also take a coordinated approach to their affairs. Some individuals specialize in different asset classes, look at various market sectors they might want to invest in, and perform tons of due diligence to ensure they're making the right decisions. These are financial analysts for the family, in a sense, and manage thousands of investments over time by using baseline or financial modeling assumptions to increase their odds of success. Others are accountants and CPAs who make sure the numbers add up and the families get the best tax treatments considering their wealth. Others might be trust or estate attorneys who keep an eye on details and current events to ensure that money is passed and protected in the best manner if something unexpected happens. This annual conference is designed to bring the largest RIAs and Family Offices to one place to discuss current topics of interest, which is important because most family offices are very fragmented and often work in silos. The conference is a way to get large families and RIAs together to network and learn about what other family offices are doing with their wealth, sometimes leading to co-investments with other family offices or RIAs to get better deal flows. One of the things I learned is that large RIAs and Family Offices like to look at private companies over public companies. Why is this? Because alternative asset classes like private equity produced average annual returns of 10.48% over the 20-year period ending on June 30, 2020, compared to the Russell 2000[9] Index, which returned 6.69%, or the S&P 500 that returned

---

9   The Russell US Indexes, from mega cap to microcap, serve as

5.91%. [10] I think what every person is looking for, whether you have wealth or not, is to do business with people they trust, which resonated with me because trust is what drives me at my core. I'm not a salesman or a wheeler-dealer. I'm a fireman turned financial adviser who is now a financial services business owner, and I want clients for life. My mission statement states that I want to be a client's last financial adviser. I speak the truth at all costs, even if it doesn't bring me the business. I think people need to hear the truth.

A multi-family office (MFO) is just that — they're made up of a handful of very successful families who have placed their wealth with a firm that understands their preferred business model and has experience in the industry. These families have come together through this conference. Many advisers want to manage these family offices because there are approximately six trillion dollars in this market. Combine that with an enormous transfer of wealth in the world happening over the next twenty-five years when approximately thirty-trillion dollars is expected to be transferred from baby boomers to the next generations. So many of these families feel that advisers and brokers are trying to work with them to get into their wallets. Still, these families don't necessarily trust these large wirehouses or brokerage firms with their money. They feel that these large companies simply want to sell their proprietary products for the related fees, and their interests aren't necessarily aligned with the families'. The primary reason this conference takes place is to bring the largest RIAs and the wealthiest families together in one place to allow a network of like-minded individuals to come to the table,

---

leading benchmarks for institutional investors. https://www.ftserussell.com/products/indices/russell-us

10   https://www.investopedia.com/ask/answers/040615/how-do-returns-private-equity-investments-compare-returns-other-types-investments.asp

shake hands, and connect, which builds economies of scale. These families just want to know they can trust the people they work with and strive to work with the best. I've seen many large wirehouses lose market share to RIAs because of their more customized approach to the clients they serve.

As a disclaimer, I started my own RIA because I saw inefficiencies in the retail broker/dealer space because I felt that I could customize individual portfolios and provide sound financial advice for anyone who needs it. Having the opportunity to attend this event opened my eyes even more and not just to the high net-worth families looking for places to come together and network. I learned that RIAs like myself could attend, shake hands with, and present our vision to these individuals. In addition, I realized that I could possibly direct investments into the identical vehicles that they utilize, which provides valuable opportunities for my existing clients and allows me to share my message with a wider audience. At the end of the day, it's about doing what I set out to do, and that is to help as many individuals and families as I can. If that entails working with a family office and providing my services, that's fantastic because I want to create the same financial opportunities for my clients as some of these families who have amassed great wealth.

CASE STUDY 4
– BEAR MARKET

SITUATION

We had an annual visit with a retired firefighter who expressed to me that she had $50,000 to invest. We learned that she read one of our monthly Savvy Investor emails and took note of one of the videos I created that talked about taking advantage of a down market. Our meeting was during the beginning of COVID 19 when the market was in a steep decline. So, I created the video to encourage clients to invest because prices were down if they had cash on hand. Well, she did, and so did her brother, who had never invested before.

CHALLENGE

There was no challenge in this situation.

OUTCOME

On April 2, 2020, we invested a total of $57,000 for both the firefighter and her brother in an equity portfolio. The purpose of this particular account was growth, and equities are a growth-oriented asset.

As of June 6, 2021, the account performed incredibly well, returning 76%. They were extremely happy with the results and appreciated the continuous education received from our monthly Savvy Investor emails. Not only that, she was ecstatic that her brother is now an investor.

My goal and vision are to help as many clients as possible, providing some of the highest-level techniques and strategies for them. It's really about creating a firm that looks at the big picture – a much more comprehensive picture than a brokerage might offer. Just like in the family office world, I need to look at things more holistically. It's not just about providing alpha or making the best investments. It's about making sure the wealth is transferred in the most tax-efficient way and, in some cases, including philanthropy down the road to benefit the client's tax obligation while improving the world as we know it. My mission is to do more impactful investing and consider things that need to be thought through now for the future Using hockey terms to bring this concept to life, it's not where the puck is now. It's where you want it to go that we have to understand.

Stock Markets Drop as Global Coronavirus Spread Continues

Daily change in closing prices of stock indices (in percent)*

Dow Jones — Nikkei — Kospi — S&P/ASX 200

-9.86
-12.18
-15.49

* Baseline/0 percent: Feb 3 closing
Source: Google Finance

COVID-19 Impact   statista

CHAPTER 13

THE PANDEMIC

AS OF THIS WRITING, I'M sitting in my office quarantined from the world like most people are right now. We've seen the COVID-19 pandemic

---

11 https://www.statista.com/chart/20942/stock-markets-glob-al-coronavirus/

handicap the country and seize life as we knew it. We've seen the market drop almost 30% from peak to trough. I have seen my gains from the last bull market in 2009-2019 nearly entirely erased in my personal accounts. People are concerned about their future and fearful of the unknown.

What lies on the other side of this pandemic? How will the economy look, and when will people go back to work? When this virus broke in Wuhan, China, little was known about how devastating it would be. There have been layoffs and a record number of people filing for unemployment. It wasn't that long ago in 2008 that something similar happened to the financial world with the stock market crash as the housing bubble burst. Many people lost their homes, jobs, and a lot of their wealth. The only difference between now and then is that in 2008, bear markets happened because banks were careless about who they loaned money to, and a silent killer is causing the volatility in 2020/2021. We need to ask, what did we learn from 2008 until now?

Individuals who play the same game year after year, continuing to invest in the market and allocate their funds in a 60-40 portfolio model, should be aware – the game in 2020 has changed. As life changes, so do investments. What works today may not work in the future. I see financial products come and go all the time. The industry is looking for vehicles that have some risk aversion built into them. It's a good strategy in many ways because it allows you to keep more of your money if the markets do go down. Things could turn out different for those who continue to play in the market with their life savings. In my twenty years with the fire department, I saw the dot. com crash, the 2008 financial crash, and now, the 2020 pandemic crash. But through all of those dips in the market, I will be able to retire from firefighting successfully, not by picking the best stocks of the moment but by exploring different vehicles that allow me to get where I want to go.

Remember, it's not all about returns. People feel the pain of losses more than they enjoy the pleasure of gains. Warren Buffet said, "It's insane to risk what you have for something you don't need." He's not a big fan of taking an excessive risk – especially when risk is not required to reach your end goal. Many people experienced tremendous growth from 2009-2019, but many of us got greedy and lost a lot of our gains. It's always a good idea to have a safety net in case something were to happen. That's why working with a fiduciary, especially one who has experience in these volatile environments, is so important. Being an investor and having lived through 2008 and 2020's real-life experiences, I've learned a lot about life and this business. I've been on this journey for twenty years now, seeing what works and what doesn't. I've seen every aspect of how people deal with adversity. It's wise to work with someone who's been a little beaten up but has come out on top. I've seen my share of misfortune which has taught me valuable life lessons and useful skills. The scars a person carries show that he's been through hell and back, is still fighting, and leading others to brighter times.

CASE STUDY 5 – BAD ADVICE

SITUATION

In their late 40s, a couple working as firefighters were concerned that they lost money in their brokerage account. The brokerage account they opened had been funded with the cash received from the sale of their home. They wanted to be very conservative with this money and protect it since they planned on using it in the next few years to build their dream home. However, their adviser placed their money in a portfolio of market stocks which lost them $60,000.

CHALLENGE

After speaking to both of them, I understood the bad experience with their previous adviser. The couple shared their goal for the $300,000 they had to invest and knew I had to gain their trust slowly. So I made sure to take my time educating them on a strategy to ensure that they understood the approach. I introduced them to Market-Linked CDs that offer conservative protection like conventional CDs, but they provide moderate growth as well because their return is based on a market index.

After a handful of visits, they both agreed they felt comfortable with the strategy and appreciated the hand-holding I provided them during the process.

OUTCOME

We see this couple on an annual basis and continue to monitor their brokerage account. They are very happy with the strategy implemented and feel they have a better understanding of the product.

If you are reading this book because you're interested in saving for retirement or creating your financial legacy, find someone to help you who watches out for you and sizes up your situation before trying to sell you something. That's what I did in my blue firefighter's uniform long before I started taking tests to get my Series 7 and Series 66 licenses. I've seen many close calls on and off the fire truck, a wrong step here or a wrong step there, even when picking stocks. That can have a massive impact on the potential success of a retirement plan and on your life as you've dreamed of living it. Every step you take in life is as important as every step I've taken and continue to take. Whether on a roof of a building during a structure fire or investing in my and my family's future – the wrong move can change everything! That's a life lesson I gladly share.

RESOURCES

FINANCIAL EDUCATION LINKS

1. 3 Worlds of Investing— https://www.youtube.com/watch?v=Ep-CeaLPxalg

2. The Fiduciary Standard— https://www.youtube.com/watch?v=pYtWrBakkVI&t=2s

3. Tax Diversification— https://www.youtube.com/watch?v=G-mldsB1evGA&t=1s

4. The Value of a Second Opinion— https://www.youtube.com/watch?v=asJhQmIMIgI&t=27s

5. What Happens to $1.00 Over Time— https://www.youtube.com/watch?v=37rfSSRYGGk

6. US Debt— https://www.usdebtclock.org/

7. Tony Robbins Explains The Meaning of a Fiduciary— https://www.youtube.com/watch?v=2i6xrNius9Y

8. Butchers v Dietitians / Brokers v Advisors / Suitability v Fiduciary— https://www.youtube.com/watch?v=AfSaENxAe0M

9. Financial Snapshot: How Will You Pay For Retirement

FIRE SAFETY LINKS

10. Home Escape Plans— https://www.phoenix.gov/fire/safety-information/home/escape

11. Fire Prevention— https://www.phoenix.gov/fire/prevention

12. CPR Training— https://www.redcross.org/take-a-class/cpr

13. Water Safety— https://www.phoenix.gov/fire/safety-information/home/water

14. Child Safety Seats— https://www.phoenix.gov/fire/safety-information/onthemove/child-seat

TIPS

Know your local/city fire department by visiting their website.

Know your emergency and non-emergency line numbers for Fire and Police.

Visit your fire station in your due area. Take a station tour. And bring them some goodies as well…they love the sweets.